Book Of Deals

The very best discounts around the world for travelers over 50.

By GENE & ADELE MALOTT
Editors of _The Mature Traveler_ Newsletter

GEM Publishing Group

The Mature Traveler's Book of Deals

Copyright © 1997 by GEM Publishing Group,
250 E. Riverview Circle, Reno, NV 89509.
<u>To Order Copies By Mail</u>: Send $7.95 plus $1.95
postage & handling.

All rights reserved. No portion of this book may be reproduced, stored in a retrieval system or transmitted by any photographic, electronic or mechanical process without written permission from the publisher, except that up to 300 words may be used in a published review of the book, with appropriate credit.

Cover design by Blue Devil Graphics, Davis, Calif.
Printed in the United States of America
ISBN 0-9629034-6-9

Contents
The Mature Traveler's Book of Deals

1. ON TURNING 50   1
Never be embarrassed to ask for the senior discount—What is a mature traveler, anyhow? —Very best deals for 49ers+—Why seniors get discounts—AARP, CARP and the others—Those travel clubs—Beware of Senior Shucks.

    Bonus: What's so great about becoming 50, anyway?

2. LODGING DEALS   9
Shopping for lodging discounts--Senior-friendly rooms--Special bargain times: Off-season, special days, late afternoon--Non-conventional lodging bargains: Homestays, retirement villas, military hotels--Lodging deals even better than seniors--More low-cost (or free) lodging deals: Campus stays, hosteling, condo rentals, home swaps.

    Bonus: Mature travelers' best inn values.

3. AIRLINE DEALS: TAKING OFF AT HALF-PRICE   31
Senior fare plans: Discounts, coupons and passports--Bereavement fares--Consolidators--Air couriers--New guys in the skies.

    Bonus: Best airline deals for seniors.

4. CRUISING ALONG AT A DISCOUNT   47
The low cost of cruising--How to find the discounts--Cruise specialists--Last-minute travel clubs--Positioning cruises--Gentleman hosts.

    Bonus: Best cruise deals for mature travelers.

5. AUTO RENTAL DEALS YOU <u>CAN</u> REFUSE   55

They don't make shopping easy—How to pay $25 a day (or less)--What to ask—When to rent.
   Bonus: Auto-rental deals for 49ers+.

6. GREAT TRAINS, GREAT MEMORIES   61

Amtrak's All-Aboard America Fares—Via Rail's Silver and Blue Service—Britrail—Eurotrains.
   Bonus: Rail deals for mature travelers.

7. SKI DEALS: HOW 49ERS+ SAVE COLD CASH   69

70-Plus Ski Club—Over The Hill Gang—Downhill deals—Cross-country—Elderhostel lessons.
   Bonus: Resorts where mature skiers save.

8. HOW SOLOS BEAT THOSE SINGLE SUPPLEMENTS   83

Why single supplements?—"The economics of meeting the overhead"—Travel matchmakers—Single-share programs—Tours just for singles—No supps at all.
   Bonus: Solo-friendly cruiselines.

9. LOW-COST AND NO-COST WAYS TO GO   93

Elderhosteling—Group tour leaders—Outdoor volunteers—Other ways to work for your supper: What's your specialty?

10. BARGAINS GALORE IN SENIORS' FAVORITE PLACES   101

Great Britain—Hawaii—New Zealand—Alaska—Caribbean—Florida—San Francisco—London—Paris—Las Vegas—New York—Seattle.
   Bonus: Vote for your favorite trip.

11. NICKELS AND DIMES: DEALS THAT ARE JUST PLAIN FUN   113

INDEX TO THE DEALS   129

1. On Turning 50: Offers You Don't Want to Refuse

Never be embarrassed to ask for the senior discount. These discounts help set us apart from the younger travelers--and save money!

The readerboard at the motel in Winnemucca, Nev., said "Rooms $55 . . . 20% Off to AARP." Well, you don't have to be a rocket scientist to figure out that an $8 membership in the American Association of Retired Persons (AARP) is a bargain if you can save $11 with it on your first night out.

With that realization, you officially become a "mature traveler." You start thinking about deals and discounts. Whether you also want to think of yourself as a "senior citizen" at that point is your business. Are word games important when compared with travel savings?

How old do you have to be to win these savings? To join AARP, CARP (its Canadian equivalent), Mature Outlook and other such clubs, you have to be 50; but you don't have to be "retired," not even "mature."

And don't avoid asking for these discounts just because you're only 40: Younger spouses sharing a trip get full AARP discounts and deals on lodging. Younger companions of fliers over 62 share many airline discounts. Younger friends go on trips packaged by Grand Circle Travel and Saga Holidays, which are usually limited to 49ers+, all the time.

What is "mature travel," anyhow? our readers often ask. And we reply:

It does not refer to travel for old people. Rather,

the mature traveler is chronologically gifted; one who's been around long enough to have the common sense to look for the very best bargains—not necessarily to save money, but to stretch the travel budget, to enjoy extra days on the road or an extra-good meal. A mature traveler is a person who qualifies for the discounts.

That's why, without a hint of embarrassment:

Wherever you travel, always ask for the senior discount.

Discounts Just for Us

Travel deals are everywhere, for everybody.

Almost any traveler, young or old, who spends enough time and knows where to look can take advantage of some kind of special deal: 21-day-advance-purchase airfares, "hidden-city" bargains, auto-rental discounts, off-season rates, twofers and the like.

With the possible exception of meals, any traveler who pays full rate on anything is probably traveling on somebody else's expense account. And even the cost of eating out in many cities can be reduced by buying a "Discount Dining Club" coupon book full of twofers, or by eating early.

As mature travelers, though, we are twice-blessed. Not only can we use the discounts that everybody else gets, but we get special discounts of our own. We just have to know where to find them.

Many travel deals for seniors are moving targets—seasonal, subject to instant cancellation or the like. Many listed as examples in this book will be gone by the time you get around to using them. For that reason, you need to subscribe to an up-to-date travel newsletter that lists current discounts for seniors. One such newsletter is _The Mature Traveler_ (monthly, $29.95 a year, P.O. Box 50400, Reno, NV 89513-0400), edited by the authors of this book.

What kind of deals are offered to mature travel-

On Turning 50

ers? Here are some of the best:

✓ Spend a winter month in Florida for under $1,000—room and meals included. (See page 21.)

✓ Stay at Rodeways, Clarions, Econo Lodges or any other Choice hotel or motel for 30% off. (See page 24.)

✓ Stay at Hiltons or Omnis at even deeper discounts—50% off or more. (Page 25, 27.)

✓ Fly across the continent for $115. (Page 39.)

✓ Or fly to Alaska for only $149. (Page 44.)

✓ Ski at half-price—or even free—at hundreds of leading North American resorts. (Page 75.)

✓ Take an Elderhostel learning trip anywhere in North America for little more than $50 a day. (Page 93.)

✓ Cruise the Caribbean—or even to Alaska—for $100 a day or less. (Page 54.)

✓ Get free admission plus half-price camping at national parks and forests. (Page 127.)

✓ Get a room on Maui for as low as $41, or on Waikiki for just a few dollars more. (Page 103.)

✓ Get good Las Vegas rooms for as low as $20-to-$30 a night—or stay a week in a one-bedroom villa for $70 a night (golf included, winnings excluded). (Pages 21, 109.)

✓ Get free admission to top French museums, half-off on French trains. (Page 107.)

✓ Sleep in Orlando's grandest hotel for $89 a night. (Page 105.)

These are the kind of deals that help you make economical travel plans.

Why Seniors Get Discounts

Even if you've just turned 50 and are coming kicking and screaming into seniorhood, never be embarrassed to ask for the discount. We don't get discounts because we're good guys, nor because we've have had the simple good luck to survive for so long. We get them because it's good business for the travel companies.

Think of it as "empty-seat theory."

Once a plane has taken off with an empty seat,

there is no way for the airline to claim any revenue for that seat. A hotel or motel cannot make any money on a room that goes empty overnight. So who will fill them?

Those who have to flexibility to travel when the hotels and planes are most empty, those not tied to school days or vacation schedules.

Those who have the yen to travel. Those who have the discretionary income to travel.

People who have been in their jobs long enough to have four weeks of vacation. Retired people. People who work part-time or for themselves. People whose mortgages are paid and don't have to support kids living at home.

Mature travelers. Us!

Travel marketers know it is a myth that seniors, living on fixed incomes, can't afford to travel long distances. They know that Americans over 50—about a quarter of the population—control more than half the nation's discretionary income and that Americans over 50 hold 40% of adult passports, spend 70% of all cruiseship dollars and take almost 75% of all recreational vehicle (RV) trips. They know that surveys show travel is the No. 1 activity favored by those about to retire.

Travel companies know mature travelers are chomping at the bit to fill their empty seats, rooms and cabins—provided they'll make us a deal better than their competitor's.

No wonder they try to get our attention by offering us discounts.

Those Travel Clubs

Forget the politics, the hard-sell insurance offers, the mail-order prescriptions and such. The truth is that mature travelers interested in getting the best discounts have to join AARP or some similar organization.

Though it has not offered trips especially for members for several years, AARP is still the leading travel-related club for seniors.

That's because the AARP card, in effect, is a union card for seniors—a universally recognized proof of age. Flash your AARP card at a motel that

On Turning 50

gives discounts for folks over 60, or at a movie theater that starts senior discounts at 65 and, even if you're only 50, chances are you'll get the discount. Rarely is the travel vendor or merchant affiliated with AARP—usually, AARP has never heard of them.

Example: You can be age 90 and still not get a decent discount on room at Marriotts. But if you show an AARP card, they'll give you 50% off. The same is true at Omni Hotels. Same for most car rentals.

Currently, an AARP family membership costs $8 a year. To get membership information, contact AARP, 601 E St. NW, Washington, DC 20049; call 202/434-2277. Canadians can contact CARP at 27 Queen St. #1304, Toronto, ON Canada M5C 2M6; call 416/363-8748.

For those who simply will not join AARP or CARP as a matter of principle, there are alternative clubs whose membership cards are also recognized as "senior ID:"

Mature Outlook—This club, sponsored by Sears Roebuck, provides people over 50 with discounts on Sears merchandise and Allstate Motor Club insurance, in addition to travel discounts that, if anything, are better than AARP's. Example: One of the perks is membership in ITC-50, a worldwide hotel-and-dining discount club. Family dues are $14.95 a year. For information, contact any Sears store or write Mature Outlook, P.O. Box 10448, Des Moines, IA 50306; call 800/336-6330.

Y.E.S. Discount Club—Sponsored by Montgomery Ward for folks over 55, this club offers benefits similar to Mature Outlook's. In addition to travel discounts, there are rebates on any trips booked through the Y.E.S. Club Travel Service. Dues are $34.99 a year. Contact Montgomery Ward Y.E.S. Discount Club, 200 N. Martingale Rd., Schaumburg, IL 60173; call 800/421-5396.

Your memberships should not end there: all RV and auto travelers should join AAA or Good Sam for the road assurance they provide. A half-price hotel club and a dining club like Preferred Travelers Club (see Chapter 2) offer great discounts on the road.

There are some seniors-only discount travel clubs, also, that you have to join <u>before</u> you hit the road in order to take advantage of their bargain rates: Hilton's SeniorHHonors Club with 50% discounts or more for guests 60+, Howard Johnson's Golden Years Club with 20%-to-50% discounts for 49ers+ and Holiday Inns' Alumni Club featuring 20% discounts for guests 50+ (see Chapter 2). They all charge annual dues, and to justify the extra cost, you need to have some brand loyalty: it's pointless to pay Hilton's $50 yearly dues if you plan to stay there only one night.

Other lodging chains' "clubs" for seniors, like Days' Inn September Club and Shoney's Merit 50 Club are not clubs at all—they are simple discount plans that, if you qualify by age, you can "join" simply by walking up to the registration desk.

Beware of Senior Shucks

Generally, travel vendors who give mature travelers discounts are trying to tell you that they are senior-friendly, that they want your business more than others'—and the discount is a token of this affection, as well as good business.

But mature travelers, in their quest for ever-deeper discounts, should be wary of "senior shucks."

A "senior shuck" is a deal in which seniors have to pay the same or more than younger travelers—while the marketing department is claiming to give a senior discount. Sometimes publications actually print these deals; then those who call for reservations at the "senior discount rate" end up paying more than anybody else.

"We love you, mature travelers, but we're going to charge you more," is what they're really saying.

Classic senior shucks are auto rental "discounts" for seniors. At many rental agencies, AARP members can get 10%-to-15% off posted rates—the full rates—at the same time travelers of any age are quoted promotional rates perhaps half off.

On Turning 50

A few years ago an international air carrier published ads offering fliers 60+ $100 off the $648 transatlantic fare between New York and Morocco. At the same time it was offering travel agents $528 fares for their clients of any age. "If I'm 60, why do I have to pay $20 more for a ticket?" we asked the airline. There was no reply.

We get a chuckle out of banks' clubs for seniors that typically list among their senior benefits "free parking." Or resorts that list among their perks "manager's cocktail reception" and "free continental breakfast." We've never been to a resort that didn't have a manager's reception for all guests at least once-a-week, and free continental breakfasts are becoming fixtures even at motels. The parking and the breakfasts and the drinks are senior shucks, too.

Unlike travel scams against seniors, which are illegal, senior shucks are simply deceitful.

Your best defense against the senior shuck is simple. First ask what is the lowest rate for this room, flight, cruise or whatever. Then, <u>after you get an answer</u>, ask:

"Now what is my senior-citizen discount." ❐

What's So Great About Becoming 50, Anyhow?

When you turn: | **Look for these deals:**

50
Get most auto-rental discounts.
Ski at half-price or less at leading resorts.
Cruise free as a "gentleman host."
Qualify for lodging discounts, some 30%-to-50% off.
Join AARP, CARP, Mature Outlook and get the "union card."
Go on Interhostel learning trips overseas.
Take trips packaged by most other seniors-only tour groups: Grand Circle, Mature Tours, Seniors Abroad and the like.

55
Take Elderhostel learning trips.
Stay at low-cost, deluxe vacation villas at retirement communities like Cooper and Sun Cities, play free golf.
Sign up for Saga Holidays trips, Road Scholar trips.

60
Become eligible for most European "pensioner" discounts on trains, hotels, tours, attractions.
Qualify for airline deals in Canada, international airline discounts.
Get discounts on Canada's Via Rail trains.
Tour the British Isles on BritRail senior cards.

62
Earn savings on all domestic airline deals: straight discounts, senior coupons, passports and the like.
Get discounts on Amtrak trains in the U.S.

65
Qualify for all European "pensioner" deals.

70
Ski free at most leading resorts.

2. Lodging Deals

> **Wherever you go, ask for your discounts, bargain like a camel merchant and you'll lay your head on a far less costly pillow than any of your peers will.**

No matter where you travel in the U.S., Canada or Mexico, never pay the full rate for a room. Ask for the senior-citizen discount, even if one isn't posted. Most major lodging chains, as well as independents, recognize seniors as a group to be courted, and give discounts accordingly—some up to 50 percent. The only exception may be classy independent hotels that cater to business travelers. But even these hotels often need mature travelers to fill their rooms on weekends and holidays—and use discounts to encourage them.

The story is different overseas, where discounts for mature travelers are less common. But often, you get deep discounts on lodgings there, anyhow, as part of your tour package.

There also is also a wide range of other choices to add adventure to your trip or cut your lodging costs: home swaps, hosted homestays and farmstays, Vacation Villas and more.

Look for Senior Discounts Everywhere

In hotels and motels in the U.S., Mexico and Canada, published senior discounts can range up to 50 percent (some Howard Johnsons, Marriotts, Hiltons), and discounts of 15-to-25 percent are common. Some chains (like Omni, Holiday Inn, Red Roof) also offer 49ers-plus discounts at their restaurants, and some let grandkids stay free in your room.

Rodeways, Econo Lodges and a few others now have "senior-friendly" rooms with subtle touches like safety showers, bedside controls for lights and TV, brighter lighting, lever-handles on doors and faucets and big-number telephone pads. Not only is there no extra charge for these rooms, but travelers 50+ get discounts ranging up to 30%. Many inns have rooms for non-smokers at no extra charge, and some for the hearing-impaired. But you have to ask for these when you make room reservations.

A few chains require you to join their clubs (Days Inn, Howard Johnson, Shoney's and the like). But you can usually fill out an application blank when you walk into the lobby and get the discount that night.

Senior-citizen discounts are not limited to chains, either. Independents are just as eager to extend special deals to mature travelers, who only have to ask for them.

Most inns simply accept your AARP or Mature Outlook card as proof you're a "senior." You are likely to save more than the $8 cost of membership in AARP the first night you're on the road.

Shopping for the Discounts

There are two ways to get bargain rates at hotels and motels:

• Make reservations at any major hotel or motel by dialing that chain's toll-free 800-number. These numbers are listed at the end of this chapter. Or:

• Show up without reservations and be prepared to bargain like a camel merchant.

In any case, do not stop at any inn that doesn't offer you at least a 10 percent seniors' discount. To be sure you're getting a real discount, ask what the regular rate is, and compare the two.

Always ask for the seniors' discount, whether or not it's posted or listed in a directory. Young or inexperienced counter people may forget to tell you about them.

Lodging Deals

When you're calling for a reservation, let the clerk know that the cost of the room is more important to you than the mountain view. Don't stop telephone shopping until you have called at least three inns everywhere you plan to visit.

Ask about special rates, and make sure the clerk quotes you the regular room price. When you get to the inn, by the way, don't hesitate to ask about a lower rate than the one you've been quoted—central reservation clerks of major chains sometimes aren't aware of special local rates or seniors' discounts.

Those Special Bargain Times

Aside from published senior citizen discounts, you can get astonishing rate reductions on lodgings if you'll go there when the hotels and motels want you there.

Off-season is one of those times. Another is on certain days when the inns are typically empty. And another time, particularly at country motels, is late in the day when the "Vacancy" sign is still lit; that's when bargaining is most effective.

Off-season—You'll never never get a break in the winter months at any of the fancy resorts in the Southwest—not even a seniors' discount. But in the summer, in places like Palm Springs, Scottsdale and Tucson, five-star resorts typically rent their $250 rooms for as little as $69-to-$89 a night. It happens in Mexico, Florida and the Caribbean, too.

Sure, mid-day temperatures in these regions are scorching—often into the 100s—but early mornings and evenings are refreshingly cool, and a dry climate like that of California's Coachella Valley, site of Palm Springs, can make even the hottest hours more bearable. You can tee off for nine holes just before dawn—snooze, swim or read when it's hottest—and get back into the outdoors (nine more holes, maybe) just before sundown.

In winter, on the other hand, mature travelers will find spectacular room discounts at Canada's grand hotels, like Quebec's Chateau Frontenac, across northern Europe and in Switzerland. Often, "winter" starts the day after kids go back to school and resort hotels are scrambling to fill their rooms.

Since you can't call every resort yourself, ask your travel agent to shop for you.

Special days—Hotels that cater to business travelers usually are empty on weekends, and mature travelers can get all kinds of good deals then. On the other hand, if you're traveling mid-week, look for deals at resort-area motels and hotels, which typically are full on weekends.

Late in the day—If you arrive at a motel late in the day, and the "Vacancy" sign is still on, you will learn what traveling salesmen have known for a long time: There is no such thing as a "regular rate," and the "business rate" is whatever you can negotiate.

Revenue from a room is lost forever if the room isn't filled, and the motel wants you there very badly. All you have to do is give the motel manager a face-saving reason to give you a discount (just make sure you're dealing with a manager, and not a mere desk clerk). Your end of the dialog should go something like this:

"How much is the room?"

"Oh, I'm an AAA member. Can't you do any better for me?"

"Well, what about your commercial rate—isn't that a better rate?" (Use the term "commercial rate" as if you know what you're talking about. Lodging chains make deals with private companies for reduced rates so that business travelers will stay there. Most inns long ago lost track of which companies they have deals with, so just mention any major company you might have been connected with once.)

Then keep going: "That's still awfully high. Don't you have a room toward the back (or on the highway, or near the ice machine)?"

Finally, when you've gotten the price of a room just as low as you possibly can, whip out your Mature Outlook or AARP card and ask with a straight face:

"My senior discount applies to that, doesn't it?"

Non-Conventional Lodging Bargains

There's no law, of course, that you have to stay at a hotel or motel. There are many other places to lay your head, including some especially for mature travelers like us:

Homestays—You can arrange low-cost homestays—and become a host for other travelers—through clubs or travel organizations that specialize in matching families to stay in each others' homes.

Typically, clubs have "host members" who are expected to offer rooms in their homes, plus breakfast and a few hours of time to orient visitors to their communities, and "non-host members," those who travel but do not make their own homes available to others. Clubs publish directories of available homestays and sometimes newsletters.

One such club, which limits membership to mature travelers, is the Affordable Travel Club, Inc. The club's organizers, John and Suzanne Miller of Gig Harbor, Wash., claim 700 members nationwide and in 18 foreign countries. Host members pay $15 single, $20 double a night when they stay in some other members' home. Non-host members pay $10 more per night. Annual dues are $50 for hosts, $90 for non-hosts. Contact the Affordable Travel Club, Inc., 6556 Snug Harbor Lane, Gig Harbor, WA 98335; call 206/858-2172.

A special bargain for mature travelers is an overseas homestay arranged by Seniors Abroad. A recent 25-day trip to typically high-priced Japan cost Seniors Abroad tour-goers less than $2,600, including airfare—little more than half what they would have paid for an escorted tour. And they shared the lives of three different Japanese host families, saw Japan through insiders' eyes and came away with a understanding of the country.

Seniors Abroad arranges winter homestays for Americans visiting New Zealand and Australia (when it's their summer), and fall homestay tours to Japan. The group also seeks Americans in all parts of the country to host visitors from overseas. Contact Seniors Abroad, 12533 Pacato Circle N., San Diego, CA 92128; call 619/485-1696.

American-International Homestays (AIH) arranges homestays for Americans with English-speaking families in 48 countries, including China and Russia. Contact AIH at P.O. Box 1754, Nederland, CO 80466; call 800/876-2048.

Or ask your travel agent to arrange a homestay or farmstay in a country where you want to become immersed in the local culture.

Retirement Villas—Travelers 55+ can stay three or four nights near popular tourist destinations at about half the cost of comparable lodgings by booking pre-retirement visits to retirement communities. Often, a free round of golf is part of the package.

These deals are designed to introduce you to places like Cooper Communities and Sun Cities. You'll spend the three or four nights, usually in a deluxe, furnished 1BR duplex within the community—at Del Webb Sun Cities they're called "Vacation Villas." In addition to golf, you'll have use of the health spa, recreation facilities, continental breakfasts and probably a reception at which you'll meet some people who live there. In return, you'll be expected to spend a few hours touring the community and hearing a sales pitch.

But the rest of the time is yours—sun in the desert around Phoenix, see the Las Vegas shows, get the mineral-bath-and-rubdown treatment at Hot Springs, Ark.

Costs are around $60 a night and up. At Sun City Palm Desert (800/533-5932), you'll pay $299 for three nights in your Vacation Villa in winter's high season, when resort rooms are going for $150-to-$250 a night; in the summer it's $115 for three nights. At Cooper Communities' Bella Vista Village (800/553-6687) in northwest Arkansas, you'll pay $50 a night. That includes the golf and other extras.

Other Cooper Communities deals are at Hot

Lodging Deals 15

Springs, Ark., Knoxville, Tenn., western South Carolina and Branson, Mo. Sun Cities Vacation Villa packages are also available in near Las Vegas, Phoenix, Sacramento, Calif., Texas Hill Country near San Antonio and Hilton Head, S.C., near Charleston.

Military hotels--Being on Waikiki, the Hale Koa is probably the best known of a dozen or so hotels around the world available to retired military personnel and their families. Rooms are as fine as anything on the beach. It has all the amenities you'd expect: good restaurant, Sunday champagne brunch, tennis, swimming pool, beach front, a Polynesian revue in the showroom—plus a PX where guests can buy goods cut-rate just by showing their military cards.

Prices, based on your rank at retirement, are about one-third to one-half of the going rates on Waikiki. An ex-private, for example, currently pays $59 for a superior room. Ocean-front roms cost privates $77, generals $109.

You have to book rooms at Hale Koa 5-to-12 months in advance. And plan to share Hale Koa with young military couples: There's an occupancy quota of 60% active-duty personnel, 40% retired. The retired quota always fills first. Call 800/367-6027.

For retired military folks who can't get into Hale Koa, there are lodgings available on the beach at Bellows Recreation Area on Oahu and semi-modern cabins on the Big Island in Volcanoes National Park—a great place for grandkids.

Other first-rate U.S. military resort hotels are in places like Seoul, Tokyo, Hong Kong, Berlin, Heidelberg and elsewhere in Europe. For a directory of them, send $13.95 to Military Living Publications, P.O. Box 23476, Falls Church, VA 22042-0347 (703/237-0203). Ask for the booklet *Temporary Military Lodgings.*

In expensive London, military retirees and their families from any NATO country get nice rooms at Waterloo district's Union Jack Club (call 011 44 0171 928-6401) and Victory Services Club

(011 44 0171 723-4474) near Marble Arch for as little as one-third the cost of comparable rooms in commercial hotels.

Lodging Deals Even Better Than Seniors'

Lodging-at-half-price directories and clubs are among travelers' best bargains—often better than senior discounts offered by lodging chains. Entertainment Publications (EP) books are the leading directories, but there are other good ones.

Some clubs also give members discounts on cruises, airline tickets, condo stays and automobile rentals.

EP's latest Entertainment/National Hotel and Dining Directory, for example, lists 3,500 U.S. inns offering EP cardholders half-price rooms, plus 2,500 restaurants offering 20% discounts. The directory costs $42.95, and with it you get a plastic membership card that indicates to registration clerks your eligibility for discounts.

As with all hotel-discount clubs, you can make advance reservations, citing your club membership for the 50% room discount, or you can simply walk in and show your card.

You cannot always get these rooms at half-off; an EP spokesman says its participating hotels agree to honor the discount if they expect 80% or less occupancy. That kind of availability test is a string on all the discount-hotel offers.

Also, you cannot use any other discounts in combination with the half-off deals. And some discount programs just for mature travelers, like Hilton's Senior HHonors Club, give seniors more than half off at some locations.

Nevertheless, mature travelers who use hotels and motels frequently, who plan their itineraries in advance and who use toll-free 800-numbers to shop for the best lodging deals, will find it useful to sign up for at least one discount club.

In addition to a national directory, EP publishes half-price directories for Europe, Canada, Mexico,

Lodging Deals   17

U.S. regions and some individual cities. Contact Entertainment Publications at 2126 Butterfield Rd., Troy, MI 48084; call 800/445-4137.

Other half-off-lodging clubs include:

Encore (Preferred Travelers Club), whose directory lists about 4,000 North American properties including 250 small inns and B&Bs, plus dining discounts. Membership is $49.95. 800/638-0930.

ITC-50, listing more than 2,500 properties nationwide, plus 1,000 restaurants that give discounts up to 49%. 800/342-0558.

Privilege Card, which claims to list 8,600 lodgings in the U.S. and abroad. Card is often given as a member benefit by groups like the National Alliance of Senior Citizens, the American Federation of Teachers and the Amateur Golfers Association International. $74.95. 800/236-9732.

More Low-Cost—Or Free—Lodging Deals

Here are some other unusual lodging arrangements that can cut mature travelers' costs:

Stay on Campus—Many college campuses open their dorms and inns to visitors at astonishingly low prices—usually half the going rates in an area, even in large cities. The *Budget Lodging Guide*, a treasure trove of information for the bargain traveler, lists more than 430 such colleges in the United States and Canada.

Example: at Minnesota's Mankato State University travelers can get private rooms for $20 (a late-summer bonus is that Mankato State is the training campus for the Minnesota Vikings, and most practices are open free to spectators). Near Kansas City, Mo., where comparable summer rooms cost $50-to-$60 a night, William Jewell College in Liberty offers tourists rooms with baths for $28.

While advance reservations are always encouraged, you can often just walk in and get these rates. For a copy of the *Budget Lodging Guide*, send $16.95 to B&J Publications, P.O. Box 5486, Fullerton, CA 92635.

Go Hosteling—Hostels are for everyone. Not

just youths. Hostels cost even less than college rooms—as low as $5 a person a night—but they're also more rustic. Facilities may be in dormitories; you may have to bring your own bedding and help others with chores from setting communal table to doing the dishes. You usually don't need reservations here, either.

The *Budget Lodging Guide* also lists U.S. hostels, as well as others around the world. For free list of reputable hostels, contact American Youth Hostels, 733 15th St. NW #840, Washington, DC 20005; call 202/783-6161.

Rent a condo. Instead of paying daily room rates, you can save money on a two-or-three-week, stay-put vacation.

Though 2BR and 3BR condo rentals can run $200 a night or more, there are some condo-rental agencies with discount programs that cut posted rental prices by 20%-to-70%. Examples: A 4BR condo near Puerto Vallarta, Mexico, was recently offered for around $800 a week; a 2BR at Panama City, Fla., for less than $900 a month.

One agency that handles condo rentals in Europe, as well as throughout America, is Condolink, 734 N. 120th St., Omaha, NE 68154; call 800/733-4445. Another, which puts together total vacation packages that can include airfare, car, a cook and airport transfer vouchers in the United States, Mexico and the Caribbean, is Creative Leisure International, 951 Transport Way, Petaluma, CA 94954; call 800/426-7367.

You can shop for your own condo using *Condo & Villa Vacations Rated Guides* by Clinton and Ellen Burr ($17 in bookstores, or send $19 to Prentice Hall Travel, 15 Columbus Circle, New York, NY 10023). The two-book series rates almost 5,000 condos on a 1-to-10 scale, has descriptive comments by the authors about 2,000 condos, and presents some extraordinary bargains. A 2BR

Lodging Deals

condo at the Kona Billfisher on Hawaii's Big Island, for example, was recently listed at only $560 a week in low season.

Swap your house—The cheapest non-traditional housing of all—free—is home swapping. Swaps can even include your auto and your country club membership for the other family's. But you have to begin setting this up long in advance of your trip.

The leading organization for home swapping, with 5,000 listings in the U.S. and abroad, is Intervac U.S., 30 Corte San Fernando, Tiburon, CA 94920 (800/756-4663). Other home-swap agencies include Vacation Exchange Club, Key West, Fla., (800/638-3841) and Trading Homes International, Hermosa Beach, Calif. (800/877-8723). ❑

Mature Travelers' Best Inn Values

Though almost every motel and hotel in North America offers some kind of senior discount, here are some individual inns around the U.S. offering exceptional deals—some exceeding 50%—for mature travelers.

✓ indicates best values for mature travelers.

Boston—49ers+ get $195 rooms at Park Plaza Hotel and Towers in Back Bay district for $121. Call 800/899-2076.

California—AARP members at San Mateo's Dunphy Hotel get $140 rooms for as little as $58. 415/573-7661 . . . Guests 55+ get half off regular $160 room rate at Pala Mesa Resort in San Diego County wine country. 800/722-4700 . . . Temecula Creek Inn, also in San Diego wine country, gives 49ers+ $110 rooms for $70. 800/962-7335 . . . Guests 55+ pay $80 for rooms that regularly cost $125-$140 a night at Erawan Garden Resort. Deal includes breakfasts and early-bird dinners. 800/234-2926 . . . 49ers+ get half-off rooms on weekdays, 25% off on weekends, at Lake Arrowhead Resort in Southern California's San Bernardino Mountains—as low as $59.50 for $120 rooms. 800/800-6792 . . . Mayfair Hotel in downtown Los Angeles gives 49ers+ $80 rooms for $65. 800/821-8682. . . Hotel Union Square in San Francisco gives guests 60+ $99 rooms for $69. Call 800/553-1900 . . .San Francisco's Sir Francis Drake gives AARP members and others 55+ $198 rooms for $119. 800/227-5480 . . . Guests 55+ get $160 rooms for $105 at Harbor Court motel, on San Francisco's waterfront. 800/346-0555.

Caribbean—Guests 55+ get $150-a-week Forever Young discounts off $1,200-$1,600 packages at most Club Meds. 800/258-2633.

Europe—Thirty SAS International Hotels give guests 65+ percentage discounts equal to their ages.

Lodging Deals

You have to fly there on SAS. 800/221-2350.

✓ **Florida**—Senior Vacation Hotels in St. Petersburg, Lakeland (near Orlando) and Bradenton offer 49ers+ long-term winter rates less than $1,000 a month—including two daily meals—except January through March, when rates are $1,300 to $1,650. Summer rates (April-Oct.) are $700/month, with two-week minimum. 800/223-8123.

Hawaii—Waikiki Parkside gives 49ers+ 30%-to-40% off room rates that regularly range from $104 to $130. 800/237-7688 . . . AARP members and other guests 60+ get 30% off—$104 rooms for $69—at Royal Garden Hotel in Waikiki. 800/367-5666 . . . Royal Lahaina Resort on Maui gives AARP members 30% off, other guests 55+ 20% off rooms that regularly run $195-$295. 800/447-6925 . . . Kauai's Coconut Beach Resort gives travelers 55+ 30% off rooms that regularly range $125-$175. 800/222-5642 . . . Also see Castle Group and Marc Resorts for other great Hawaii discounts.

Lake Tahoe—Inn by the Lake at South Tahoe, across the street from the lake and 1-1/2 miles from casinos, gives AARP members 25% off rooms that regularly run $100-$140. 800/877-1466.

Las Vegas—Guests 55+ get $91 rooms for $63 at Bally's Las Vegas on center-Strip. 800/634-3434 . . . "Sunrise Senior Club" members get $59-$79 rooms for $39 at Melrose Suites hotel. Call 800/362-4040 to join the club; membership is free.

✓ **Fitzgerald's Casino/Hotel downtown offers guests 55+ deep room discounts—as much as 80% off—which vary by season. Example: $64-$190 rooms as low as $30 (double) in January. 800/274-5825 for current deals. The hotel includes 33 rooms for the disabled.**

New Orleans—Guests 50+ get half off weekdays, 15% off weekends, on $165 rooms at Hotel De La Poste in the French Quarter during the city's sizzling summers, June 15-Sept. 15--and sometimes during yearend holiday season. Ask for "Senior Advantage" rate. 800/448-4927.

✓ **New York**—Guests 60+ get $209 rooms for $129 at Novotel. 800/221-4542.

Puerto Rico—San Juan's Hotel Condado Beach and sister hotel, La Concho, offer 25% discounts on $158 rooms year-round for travelers 55+. 800/468-2775.

San Antonio—Historic Menger Hotel in downtown San Antonio gives guests 55+ $132 rooms for $80. Call 800/345-9285.

✓ **Toronto—AARP and CARP members get $110 (U.S.) city-view rooms for $70 at Sky Dome Hotel (part of the complex where the Blue Jays play baseball). Others 65+ get 25% discounts. 800/341-1161 or 416/341-8990.**

Switzerland—More than 380 hotels in 160 Swiss towns offer off-season rates for women over 62, men over 65. Get information from Swiss National Tourist Office, 608 Fifth Ave., New York, NY 10022; call 212/757-5944. Book through your travel agent.

Seattle—AARP and CARP members stay at Warwick Hotel for $123.50 a night, one-third off regular $190 room rates. 800/426-9280.

Lodging Deals 23

Lodging Groups' Best Deals for 49ers+

Here are hotel chains' best discounts for 49ers+. While discounts listed here were in effect at press time, all senior-discount programs are subject to change without notice. All are dependent on availability of rooms at the discounted rate. Some inns allocate as few as 2% of their rooms to senior-discount programs. When those rooms are gone, the senior discount is not available.

✓ indicates best values for mature travelers.

Admiral Benbow Inns—Chain in South and Southeast gives travelers 60+ 10% discounts. 800/451-1986.

Aston Resorts—"Sun Club" members 55+ get room discounts of 25%, plus 10% a day off auto rentals, at 40 Astons on Hawaii's major islands. Enroll at any Aston. 800/922-7866.

Best Inns—Midwestern group gives AARP members $5 discounts weekdays, $10 Sunday nights. Call 800/237-8466.

Best Western—AARP members and others 55+ get 10%-to-15% discounts. 800/528-1234.

Budgetel—Guests 55+ get 10% discounts. Call 800/428-3438.

Calinda—Inns throughout Mexico, affiliated with Choice Hotels, offer guests 50+ Senior Saver discounts of 10% to 30%, plus meal deals at some locations. See Choice Hotels. 800/228-5151.

Canadian Pacific—Grand hotels and resorts across Canada give AARP and CARP members 30% off regular rates. Others 65+ get 25% off. 800/441-1414.

✓ **Castle Resorts and Hawaiian Pacific**—Spectacular values at hotels and condos for mature travelers visiting the islands—as low as $43 a night on Maui. That rate, which reflects a $10 discount for guests 50+ from the regular $53 room charge, is for the Maui Palms hotel, near Kahului Airport. Other properties give 49ers+ 25% off $120-$140 rooms on Kauai, on Waikiki Beach in Honolulu and other islands. Mature travelers get rental cars with unlimited mileage for an extra $20 a day. For a brochure about all properties write Hawaiian Pacific Resorts, 1150 S. King St., Honolulu, HI 96814; 800/367-5004.

✓ **Choice Hotels**—Travelers 50+ get 30% off regular room rates with advance reservations, 10% without reservations. Ask for "Senior Saver Discounts" at more than 2,800 inns under the brands Comfort, Quality, Clarion, Sleep, Rodeway, Econo Lodge and Friendship, plus Calinda in Mexico. Discounts are on a capacity-controlled basis, which means only a few rooms are set aside at each Choice property each night for this discount program. Best advice: reserve months in advance to get this discount at popular vacation areas. Call 800/424-4777 for Econo Lodges, Rodeways, Friendship Inns; 800/228-5151 for Calinda; 800/221-2222 for the others.

Clarion—Senior Saver discounts of 10% to 30% for travelers 50+, plus meal discounts at some locations. See Choice Hotels. 800/221-2222.

Colony Hotels & Resorts—Motels on U.S. mainland, Israel, Russia, Thailand, Mexico and five Hawaiian islands give 10%-to-20% discounts to guests 60+. Call 800/777-1700.

Comfort Inns—Senior Saver discounts of 10% to 30% for travelers 50+, plus meal discounts at some locations. See Choice Hotels. 800/221-2222.

Conrad Hotels—Overseas hotels participate in Senior HHonors program. See Hilton Hotels.

Country Hearth—Motels in South and Southeast U.S. give 10% off regular rates to 49ers+. 800/848-5767.

Country Inns—Motels in Upper Midwest give 10%-to-20% off regular rates to guests 55+. 800/456-4000.

Courtyard by Marriott—AARP and CARP members get 10% discounts. 800/321-2211.

Cross Country Inns—AARP members and others 60+ get 25% off at 25 inns in Ohio, Michigan and Kentucky. 800/621-1429.

Lodging Deals

Crown Sterling Suites—Chain of all-suite hotels has Senior Savings Time deal that gives guests 60+ discounts ranging up to 40%. Example: Mature travelers pay $99 weekends, $109 weekdays, for $179 rooms at at Crown Sterling in Birmingham, Ala. 800/433-4600.

Days Inns—September Days Club has discounts of 15% to 40% for 49ers-plus, and also discounts on car rentals and local attractions. Get club application at any Days Inn or call September Days Club, 800/241-5050. Membership costs $15 a year. Non-members who belong to AARP get 10% room discounts. 800/329-7466 for reservations (from Canada, 800/964-3434).

Doubletree Inns & Guest Quarters—AARP members and others 65+ get 10% to 30% off rooms and full breakfasts. 800/222-8733.

Drury Inns—Low-cost chain in Midlands and the South gives 49ers+ 10% off room rates. 800/325-8300.

Econo Lodges and Econo-Travel Motor Hotels—Senior Saver rates of 10% to 30% off for travelers 50+, plus meal discounts at some locations. All Econos offer some "senior-friendly rooms." See Choice Hotels. 800/424-4777.

Economy Inns of America—Small chain in California and the South gives AARP members 10% off rates. 800/826-0778

Embassy Suites—Guests 62+ get small discounts for two-room suites. 800/362-2779.

Excel Inns—Midwest chain gives 10% discounts to guests 55+. 800/356-8013.

Fairfield Inns by Marriott—AARP and CARP members get 10% discounts on rooms that average less than $40 a night. 800/228-2800.

Friendship Inns—Senior Saver rates of 10% to 30% off for travelers 50+, plus meal discounts at some locations. See Choice Hotels. 800/221-2222.

Guest Quarters—See Doubletree.

Harley Hotels—AARP members get 10% off at 14 properties in Northeast U.S. 800/321-2323.

Hawaiian Pacific Resorts—See Castle Resorts.

✓ **Hilton Hotels—Senior HHonors Club for those 60+ entitles members to lodging discounts of 25% to 50% at more than 330 participating Hiltons, including overseas Conrad Hotels. Members also get 20% off** at many Hilton restaurants, discounts on Hertz car rentals, special frequent-stayer perks and others worth an estimated additional 2% to 5%. Dues are $50 a year, $285 for lifetime. <u>You must enroll before your trip.</u> For an application, contact Hilton Senior HHonors Service Center, P.O. Box 603, Addison, TX 75001, or call 800/432-3600. Hilton says allow three weeks for processing.

Hilton International—Senior Passport program gives travelers 60+ room discounts of 25% to 50% at 130 Hilton Hotels in 43 countries, plus three Vista Hotels in the U.S. No club membership required. 800/445-8667. (At press time, Hilton Hotels had just announced a consolidation with Hilton International. A Hilton spokesman said both chains' senior discount programs would be revised "to reflect the Baby Boomers' needs.")

Holiday Inns—"Alumni Club" members 50+ get 20% discounts on regular room rates, 10% off meals at North American Holidays. Membership fee is $10. Join before your trip—call 800/258-6642. AARP members get 10% room discounts. For reservations call 800/465-4329.

Homewood Suites—AARP members get 10% off rates for apartment-style suites. 800/225-5466.

Howard Johnson—Golden Years Club gives 15%-to-50% discounts to guests 50+ at 650+ HoJos and Plaza Hotels in U.S., Canada, Mexico, Puerto Rico, plus discounts on meals and rental cars. Membership is $12.95/year; no charge for spouses. For an application call 800/547-7829.

Hyatt—Guests 62+ get 25% or more off room rates, plus meal discounts at some hotels. 800/233-1234.

Inn Suites—Seven motels in Southwest gives 49ers+ 10% off room rates. 800/842-4242.

Innkeeper—Motels in Virginia and North Carolina give 49ers+ 10% discounts. 800/822-9899.

Kimpton Group—The Kimpton Group, with 14 hotels in San Francisco and others in Los Angeles, Portland, Seattle and Tacoma, Wash., posts discounts ranging up to one-third off room rates for AARP members and other guests 55+. There are also special packages, like "Senior Memories" at the Sir Francis Drake that includes dancing at the Starlight Room atop the hotel. Most Kimptons have daily complimentary wine

Lodging Deals

tastings. Contact each hotel separately. Best deals are at the Sir Francis Drake (800/227-5480), where $198 rooms cost seniors $119 to $139—up to 40% off; the Harbor Court (800/346-0555) on the waterfront, with $160 rooms for $105; the Monticello Inn (800/669-7777), with $139 rooms for $96 ; and the Prescott (800/283-7311), offering $215 rooms for $145.

In Los Angeles, Kimpton's Beverly Prescott (800/421-3212) offers seniors $190 rooms for $140. In Seattle, the Alexis Hotel (800/426-7033) gives visitors 55+ $20-to-$60 off $155-$300 rooms (a deal that includes evening sherry, passes to the Seattle Art Museum and a ban on tipping). And the Hotel Vintage Park (800/624-4433) offers $175 rooms for $125.

In Tacoma, Kimpton's Sheraton Tacoma (800/325-3535) gives seniors 22% off $143 rooms. Portland's Vintage Plaza (800/243-0555), gives seniors $155 rooms for $125.

Knights Inns—Budget motel chain with more than 200 properties, mostly in the East and South, gives 49ers+ 10% discounts. 800/722-7220.

La Quinta Motor Inns—Travelers 55+ get 10% discounts. 800/531-5900.

Lodgekeeper and LK Inns—Midwest chain gives 10% AARP members, others 62+ 10% off. 800/282-5711.

Marc Resorts—Hawaii chain gives 25% off or more to guests 55+, except during holiday blackouts. 800/535-0085.

Marriott—AARP members get half off posted rates with 21-day non-cancellable, non-refundable advance reservations at most Marriotts, 10% without reservations. 49ers+ get 20% off at Marriott restaurants, 10% off at gift shops. 800/228-9290.

Motel 6—AARP members get 10% discounts. Call 800/440-6000.

Novotel—Guests 60+ get discounts of one-third or more off at hotels in Canada, New York, New Jersey. 800/221-4542.

✓ **Omni Hotels—45 upscale hotels, mostly in the East and South, give discounts of 50% or more to AARP members, plus 15% off meals. Example: Cincinnati Omni gives seniors $205 rooms for $100. 800/843-6664.**

Outrigger—Hotels throughout the Hawaiian Islands, including 22 on Waikiki and the Royal Waikoloan on the Big Island's Kohala Coast, give travelers 50+ 20% off room rates. AARP members get 25% off. 800/462-6262.

Park Inns—Chain of 71 hotels throughout U.S. gives AARP members and others 60+ 10% discounts. 800/437-7275.

Quality International—Senior Saver discounts of 10% to 30% for travelers 50+, plus meal discounts at some locations. See Choice Hotels. 800/221-2222.

Radisson Hotels—More than 100 Radissons in North America guarantee 49ers+ discounts of at least 25%—more at some properties. 800/333-3333.

✓ Ramada—Best Years Club members 60+ get 25% discounts at almost 700 U.S. properties, plus frequent-stayer points that add additional free lodging, rental-car discounts, airline tickets and merchandise. Lifetime membership is $15. To join call 800/766-2378. For similar programs at Canadian Ramadas, call 800/854-7854.

Ramada International—Guests 55+ get 25% off room rates at overseas Ramadas. 800/854-7854.

Red Lion Inns—AARP members get 10% off rooms and 10% off at some restaurants. New owner Doubletree Inns may upgrade this program soon. 800/547-8010.

Red Roof Inns—RediCard Plus-60 Club gives guests 60+ 10% off rooms and deals on rental cars, restaurants, at 200 budget inns in the Midwest and East. Lifetime membership is $10. You can join when you check in. 800/843-7663.

Renaissance Hotels & Resorts—AARP members and other travelers 60+ get 25% or more off rates at luxury hotels in U.S. and Mexico. 800-468-3571.

Residence Inns by Marriott—Nationwide all-suite chain gives 15% off regular rates to AARP and CARP members. 800/331-3131.

Rodeway Inns—Travelers 50+ get 10%-to-30% discounts under Choice Hotels' Senior Saver plan. Rodeway offers senior-friendly rooms. 800/424-4777.

Sandman Motels—20 motels in western Canada give travelers 55+ 25% discounts. For free Club 55 card write 1755 W. Broadway #310, Vancouver, BC V6J 4S5

Lodging Deals

Canada. 800/726-3626.

Sheraton Hotels—More than 460 Sheratons worldwide give travelers 59+ and members of recognized senior organizations discounts of 25%. Discounts are also good at Sheraton resorts like the Desert Inn in Las Vegas, the Royal Hawaiian and Moana Surfrider on Waikiki. Sheraton advises that "some regular promotional rates are lower than seniors' rates." 800/325-3535.

Shilo Inns—Northwest U.S. chain gives 10% discounts to guests 60+. 800/222-2244 (from Canada, 800/228-4499).

Shoney's Inns—Members of free Merit 50 Club get 10%-to-15% discounts. 800/222-2222.

Sleep Inns—Senior Saver rates of 10%-to-30% off for travelers 50+, plus meal discounts at some locations. See Choice Hotels. 800/221-2222.

Summerfield Suites—Guests 62+ get discounts of 25%-to-30% at most locations. 800/833-4353.

Susse Chalets—East Coast chain gives guests 60+ 10% off rates. 800/258-1980.

Travelodge—More than 500 inns in North America give 15% unrestricted discounts (no blackout dates, no advance reservations required) to 49ers+. Call 800/545-6343.

Vagabond Inns—38 Vagabond Inns in western U.S. offer Club 55 members 15% or more off single room rates—but seniors can stay up to four in a room—plus discounts on trips and social events. 800/522-1555.

Welcome Inns—Eastern Canada chain gives token discounts to travelers 60+. 800/387-4381.

Westin Hotels—United Air Lines Silver Wings members 60+ get 50% discounts at most Westins. Call 800/228-3000.

Wyndham Hotels & Resorts—U.S. properties give AARP members and others 62+ half-off room rates. At Caribbean resorts, discounts range up to 20%. Call 800/996-3426 (from Canada, 800/631-4200).

3. Airline Deals: Taking Off for Half Price

Some passengers pay triple; some pay half. Savvy mature travelers can get the cheapest seats of all.

Airline passengers rarely compare notes about how much they paid for their seats—most would find it too embarrassing.

With your $400 round-trip ticket to Chicago, you could be sitting with a grandfather visiting his kids whose fare came to only $298 on a senior-discount coupon; or with a good shopper whose consolidator ticket cost just $200, or with a volunteer air courier whose whole flight back from Singapore, including the Chicago leg, cost little over $150.

Indeed, there are almost as many different airfares for a given flight as there are seats on the plane. But airlines give mature travelers the edge in their constant fare wars because we may be the only fliers whose travel plans can be flexible enough to fill the empty seats when the airline needs them to be filled.

And the best bargains of all go to mature travelers who can make travel plans up to a year in advance, who shop well—or those who have reliable travel agents who do the shopping for them.

Senior Discounts

There are basically two kinds of airline discount plans: flat discounts off full fares and senior-discount coupons. Discounts—usually 10%—are offered passengers as young as 60, but mostly 62+. and their companions of any age. The discounts usually apply to all published fares—full coach fares or advance-purchase fares—but not to short-time promotional fares. These sale fares are often lower than senior fares.

To make the comparison, always ask for "the lowest fare available" to the place you'll be visiting, as well as asking for the "senior-discount fare."

Many airlines permit younger companions to fly with you at the discounted rate—this is for spouses or other adult family members. Grandchildren's fares are often half-price. Frequent-flier points are awarded to those using senior discounts.

All senior-discount deals apply on airlines' partner-feeder routes, as well—but not on shuttles, which have separate senior-discount programs.

Some airlines, like Southwest, don't give regular senior discounts but post frequent seniors-only promotional fares between two pairs of cities.

International Discounts

Travelers as young as 55 also get discounts on international airlines' fares, usually about 10%, but sale fares are almost always lower. Example: El Al's liberal 15% discount for travelers 60+ and their companions 55+ is based on full New York-Tel Aviv coach fare, recently posted at $1,330—a senior rate of $1,131. But a sale fare of $949 was also advertised for passengers of any age.

Coupons and Passports

Airline passengers 62+ can buy books of four-to-eight coupons for a fixed price that can amount to as little as $230 for a round-trip flight almost anywhere in America.

Airline "passports" for mature travelers who live in selected cities cost even less: as little as $80 a round-trip!

The coupons are bargains for mature travelers who know they'll be flying to a particular city more than once a year—to visit relatives, see the shows, visit the casinos—whatever.

Airline Deals

Generally, each coupon can be redeemed for a one-way ticket anywhere the airline flies in North America—a round-trip takes two coupons. Some longer legs take two coupons—from the mainland to Hawaii, for example.

Some coupons require you to complete your trips within the year; others simply require you to redeem your coupon for a ticket and make reservations within the year, and then allow another year for you to actually travel. With a few exceptions, coupons for younger companions are not available. You have to use the coupons yourself—they are non-transferable.

You can buy senior-discount coupons from your travel agent or at airline ticketing desks. Most airlines require you to redeem coupons for tickets 14 days or more before your flight; most also permit stand-by travel. You get frequent-flier points when you fly on coupons.

Airline "Passports," which give discounts of two-thirds or more off regular fares, are offered by only one airline, Continental, for parapatetic travelers 62+ who can fly up to once each week for four months to a year.

Before you buy senior-discount coupons or passports, plan your travels carefully. Remember that you have to be traveling between two points served conveniently by the airline. You can't take advantage of TWA's low-cost coupons if you live in Phoenix, for instance; TWA doesn't go there, and you'd have to buy an extra ticket to fly to a connecting point.

Don't buy a Continental Freedom Passport for regular trips between Seattle and Los Angeles; while Continental serves both cities, there are no direct flights. You'd need an extra half-day in the air flying to Continental's hubs in Houston or Denver and back.

Do not use senior-discount coupons, either, if you're flying only short distances, because the coupon cost is fixed. Flying from Los Angeles to Las Vegas costs the same as flight from L.A. to New York. With L.A.-L.V. airfares sometimes lower than

$100, it would not be worthwhile to use two discount coupons which, in effect, cost $272.

Bereavement Fares

Most domestic airlines offer bereavement fares—not discounts. Some airlines refer to these as "compassion fares."

Rules vary slightly among airlines. Generally, either death or an illness serious enough to require hospitalization of a close family member will qualify you for a bereavement fare. The airlines ask you the name of the funeral home or of the hospital, and often will call to check.

Usually, bereavement fares are about the same as seven-day advance-purchase fares. A recent round-trip bereavement fare on American Airlines between Dallas and Kansas City, for example, was $258, compared with seven-day fare of $268. Full coach fare was $478.

You probably can get the bereavement fare you need on very short notice—there are a fixed number of seats on each flight allocated to bereavement fares, but these are seldom booked, according to a Continental Airlines spokesmen.

Consolidators

Mature travelers hunting for airfare bargains should look beyond senior discounts, passports and coupon packs to consolidators, who sometimes sell tickets at less than half the cost of regular fares.

Consolidator fares vary widely, and fluctuate from day-to-day. But they're always bargains:

On an ordinary day, one Los Angeles consolidator was advertising round-trip flights to Mexico City for $199, to Paris for $475, to Tokyo for $545. Another had round-trip tickets to Hawaii for $215, to New York for $235 and to Chicago for $187— less than half the cost of posted coach fares.

These are real seats on real airlines; the person sitting beside you on your $215 L.A.-Honolulu flight may have paid $400 to $500 for the seat. You even earn frequent-flyer points.

There is one "super consolidator" that sells

Airline Deals

tickets on TWA flights anywhere for 20% off whatever fare TWA quotes.

Consolidators, in effect, conduct the airlines' fire sales—filling seats the airlines do not expect to fill at regular fares, or even at most promotional fares, which are usually instituted to cut-rate a competitor airline. It is rare when an airline's advertised sale fare will come in below a consolidator's. Often a consolidator's fare will beat any deal mature travelers can get with senior discounts or senior coupons.

Example: For a round-trip ticket between Los Angeles and Chicago with 21-day advance purchase, United Airlines recently quoted a coach fare of $299—with United's 10% senior discount, $270. Flying with United's "Silverpack Coupons," the ticket would have cost $271.

At the same time, TWA was quoting a sale fare between L.A. and Chicago at $212. Passengers 62+ traveling on TWA's "Senior Travel Pak" coupons would have paid $249.

But you could have gotten that same seat on the same TWA flight from a Los Angeles consolidator called "Cheap Tickets, Inc." (800/377-1000) for $206, or from another consolidator, "Cheap Seats" (800/451-7200) for $197.

Even so, the "super consolidator," Global Discount Travel Services of Las Vegas, did even better, quoting $172.40 for the L.A.-Chicago round-trip—a $127 saving for the same seat on the same TWA flight for which other airlines were charging $299.

Global Discount is unique among consolidators and can sell tickets only on TWA. When TWA wanted to part company with financier Carl Icahn, known as a business raider, it agreed as part of the buyout to give him $610 million worth of tickets that he could resell at discount prices. That instantly put Icahn in the consolidator business. Global Travel has eight years to sell those TWA tickets and is doing so at 20% off whatever price TWA asks.

The best prices on consolidator tickets are for overseas flights or flights you need to take on short notice: A consolidator's ticket price will almost always beat that of an airline's bereavement fare, for example. Usually, a consolidator will not even offer a ticket that costs less than $200, because there is little profit margin there. Some consolidators deal only in international flights.

Consolidators operate mostly in large cities, and you cannot necessarily tell from a phone directory listing whether a travel agency is a consolidator. But consolidator ads appear in travel sections of big-city Sunday newspapers. All have toll-free 800 numbers, and you can deal with them from anywhere in the country—it makes no difference where you live or where the consolidator's office is located. Many consolidators offer to send tickets by Federal Express.

Consolidators are handicapped by their agreement with airlines that they cannot advertise the name of the airline—just the price. When you call in response to an ad however, they can tell you the airline you'll be flying on.

Always charge consolidator tickets on your credit card—never send cash or a check. You'll be dealing with companies you've never heard of, and there are some fly-by-nights in the consolidator business. Should you okay credit-card payment and your consolidator tickets not arrive, the credit-card company will refund your money on grounds of non-fulfillment.

Some travel agents will check out consolidator fares for you—but others will not. Those agents feel that because consolidator tickets cost less, they earn lower commissions. On the other hand, others are eager to deal with consolidators because there is no commission cap on consolidator tickets—they could earn higher commissions than an airline would pay. Many consolidators will not sell tickets

Airline Deals

to individuals—only travel agents.

If you are buying your own consolidator tickets, telephone-shop from among these leading consolidators: Air Tickets (800/207/7300); Cheap Seats (800/451-7200); Cheap Tickets, Inc. (800/377-1000); Euram (800/848-6789); Europak Scan (800/253-1342); Global Discount Travel Services (800/497-6678); Jetset (800/638-3273); Skylink (800/247-6659); Travac (800/872-8800).

Air Couriers

Mature travelers who can travel on short notice save 75% or more on international airfares by acting as air couriers.

One courier recently flew from Los Angeles to Singapore, with a stopover in Tokyo, for $150 round-trip. At the same time a consolidator was quoting an L.A.-Singapore round trip at $739. An L.A.-Bangkok round-trip ticket, quoted by a consolidator at $739, cost an air courier just $275 late last year.

The catches are that you can take only carry-on baggage, you have to go when the courier service wants you to go and it's difficult to take anybody with you.

Another disadvantage is that courier services operate from international gateways like New York, Miami, Chicago, Los Angeles and Montreal. Mature travelers who don't live in one of these places could spend more getting to them than any savings resulting from the discount airfares.

In return for discounted tickets, a courier carries baggage for companies that need to get goods around the world in a hurry: film rushes, documents, computerized data and the like.

To keep track of available courier flights, mature travelers can join one of two associations that offer members the same type of services: lists of air-courier firms with addresses, bi-monthly bulletins listing available courier flights, daily updates by fax and a bi-monthly newsletter.

The International Association of Air Travel

Couriers charges members $45 a year. Write IAATC at P.O. Box 1349, Lake Worth, FL 33460; call 407/582-8320. Membership in the new Air Courier Association, based in Denver, costs $58 the first year, $28 after that. For information and an enrollment kit call 303/278-8810.

New Guys in the Skies

The skies are full of new airlines whose aim is to take you from Point A to Point B cheaper than the big guys can. These no-frills airlines can mean bargains for mature travelers.

Some serve smaller destinations the big guys won't touch—Branson, Mo., Myrtle Beach, S.C., Minot, N.D. and so on. Most have no on-board meals, no movies, no drinks, no baggage transfer. That's why their fares can be lower and why only a few (Kiwi International, Reno Air, Frontier) can offer senior discounts.

While these airlines may quote fares lower than you can get elsewhere, mature travelers also should consider the airline's safety record, reliability (late starts, flight cancellations, etc.) and the age of its planes. All of these elements are part of the public record, and your travel agent should be able to find the information. ❏

Airline Deals

Best Domestic Airline Deals For Mature Travelers

Here are domestic air carriers' discount programs for mature travelers. Be aware that quoted rates can change almost daily.

✓ indicates best values for mature travelers.

• **Air Canada**—Gives 10% discounts to fliers 60+ and their companions of any age on cross-Canada flights and flights between Canada and U.S. gateways, including Florida. Airline offers no discount coupons. 800/776-3000.

• **Alaska Airlines**—Gives 10% discounts to passengers 62+ and their companions of any age. Call 800/426-0333.

• **America West**—Passengers 62+ and younger companions get 10% discounts off published fares.

✓ Passengers 65+ get even deeper discounts on selected routes. Example: Posted Reno-Phoenix round-trip fare of $134 is reduced to $121.50 for passengers 62+, to $106 for those 65+—a 20% saving.

✓ Senior Saver Pack coupons for passengers 62+ are priced considerably below those of most other U.S. airlines: $495 for four coupons, $920 for eight, making a round-trip between any American West city pair $230.

Mexico City flights require two coupons for each leg. Restrictions make these coupons harder to use than most others: There is a long list of blackout dates. You may use coupons only for flights from noon Mondays through noon Thursdays or all day Saturdays; 14-day advance purchase is required, though stand-by is allowed. You have one year to fly on your Senior Saver Pack coupon. 800/235-9292.

- **American Airlines**—Passengers 62+ and their traveling companions of any age get 10% discounts off published fares.

Senior SAAver coupon books for travelers 62+ cost $596 for four coupons: a round-trip cost to seniors of $298 between any mainland cities served by American, plus Puerto Rico (midweek only) and the U.S. Virgin Islands. Hawaii flights take two coupons each way, and coupons cannot be used on flights to Alaska. You must redeem coupons within one year, but you have another year to complete travel. Coupons are valid any day; make reservations 14 days in advance, but stand-by is allowed. 800/237-7981.

- **Canadian Airlines**—Gives passengers 60+ and their companions of any age 10% discounts on lowest available fares. Canadian Airlines does not offer senior coupons. 800/426-7000 (from U.S.), 800/665-1177 (from Canada).

- **Continental Airlines**—Travelers 62+ and companions get 10% discounts.

Continental Freedom Trips coupons for travelers 62+ cost $579 for books of four, $999 for books of eight—at $250 per round-trip, slightly less than most airlines' coupons. There are no companion coupons. Flights between any Continental cities on the mainland take one coupon each way; Anchorage, Hawaii, Mexico and Caribbean flights require two coupons. You must redeem coupons for tickets within one year, but you have another year to complete travel. Coupons can be used any day; 14-day advance purchase is required, but stand-by is permitted.

In addition, several Continental Freedom Passport programs offer even better discounts for travelers 62+ who fly a lot. Younger travel companions may buy passports at the same prices:

Domestic Freedom Passport costs $1,999 for a full year in coach, $3,499 for first class. The passport is good for one leg each week (not one round trip) between 80 Continental cities on the U.S. mainland and Vancouver, B.C.—that works out to less than $80 a

Airline Deals

round trip, if you use all of them. <u>Serious restrictions make "passports" hard to use</u>: You must fly between noon Mondays and noon Thursdays or on Saturdays, and stay over a Saturday night. There is a limit of three trips a year to each destination. You cannot make reservations until seven days before your trip—another serious limitation, since seats allocated to this program are relatively scarce.

✓ Four-month Domestic Freedom Passport costs $999—$118 a round-trip—and permits one-way travel once a week for just four months from purchase date anywhere on Continental's domestic system. This is a much more useful deal, though the same restrictions apply. Younger companions may also buy Passports at these prices.

Global Coach Traveler Passport, which costs $4,499 a year, allows 48 legs (24 round trips) between Continental cities, including two round-trips to Mexico and the Caribbean; one each to Alaska, Central America, Europe, Hawaii and the South Seas. Remainder of the trips must be domestic. First-class Global Passport is $6,999. You can make reservations up to 21 days in advance. 800/441-1135.

• **Delta Air Lines**—Fliers 62+ and younger companions get 10% off all posted fares. Young At Heart coupons for those 62+ cost $596 for four--a round-trip cost of $298. Hawaii and Alaska round-trip flights require four coupons. There are no coupons for younger companions. Travel is permitted any day, and there are no blackout dates. You have to make reservations 14 days in advance, though stand-by is permitted, and fly within a year of the coupon purchase date. Call 800/221-1212.

• **Delta Shuttle**—Fliers 62+ pay $140 weekdays for two-way commutes between Boston, New York, Washington that regularly cost $300. You have to fly between 10:30 a.m. and 2:30 p.m. Mondays through Fridays, or between 7:30 and 9:30 p.m. No reservations—just show up at the gate.

✓ Flight Pack Coupons for shuttle passengers 62+ cost $227 for four, $418 for eight, plus airport

fees—a round-trip cost of $104.50, 30% below the next-best senior fare. No companion coupons. 800/221-1212.

• **Frontier Airline**—New Denver-based carrier, flying to smaller cities in West and Northwest, gives 10% discounts to passengers 62+ and their companions of any age. 800/432-1359.

• **Hawaiian Air**—Passengers 60+ and their traveling companions of any age get 10% off most fares from the mainland to Honolulu and South Pacific points—but no longer on inter-island shuttle flights. There is no senior coupon program. Call 800/367-5320 (from Honolulu, 838-1555).

• **Kiwi International Airlines**—Regional airline flies between New York, Chicago-Midway, Atlanta, Tampa, Orlando, West Palm Beach—and Las Vegas. Despite its name, there are no international flights.

✓ **Passengers 62+ and their companions of any age get 20% discounts on posted fares.**

✓ **Kiwi's six-coupon Senior Discount Pack costs $678, making a round-trip between Kiwi cities $223. Companions of any age may also buy Senior Discount Packs.**

Coupons are valid any day. Make reservations seven days or less before departure. You have one year to fly with the coupons. 800/538-5494.

• **Lone Star Airlines**—Regional carrier flying to smaller Midwest cities from Dallas/Fort Worth gives travelers 62+ 10% off posted fares. No companion discounts. 800/877-3932.

• **Midwest Express**—Passengers 62+, but not companions, get 10% off all published fares. There is no senior coupon program. Midwest flies out of Milwaukee to Midwestern, East and West coast points. Call 800/452-2022.

• **Northwest Airlines**—Gives 10% discounts to fliers 62+ and their companions of any age on most fares. NorthBest Senior Coupons cost $596 for four—a round-trip cost of $298 between any Northwest mainland cities. It takes two coupons to fly to Anchorage or Honolulu—

Airline Deals

total of four for a round-trip. You must redeem coupons for tickets within one year, but you have another year to complete travel. Fourteen-day advance booking is required, but stand-by is allowed. Coupons are valid any day. 800/225-2525.

• **Reno Air**—Low-cost carrier serving mostly Western cities, plus Chicago and Detroit, gives passengers 62+ and their younger companions 10% off all posted fares, deeper discounts on selected routes. Example: Regular Los Angeles-Seattle fare is $196; seniors fly for $158—a 20% saving. There is no senior-coupon program. 800/736-6247.

• **Southwest Airlines**—Offers discounts to travelers 65+ that vary from city-to-city and change frequently. Though the airline guarantees no other promotional fare will be lower than seniors' fares, many are exactly the same, and there are no companion discounts.

Southwest's "Friends Fly Free" program, recently reinstated, provides cheaper fares than most Southwest senior fares if you'e flying with a companion: $396 round-trip fare ($198 a person) between Phoenix and Chicago, for instance, compared with Southwest's best posted senior fare of $258. Beware that this is an off-and-on program, not always available on all Southwest routes. 800/435-9792.

• **TWA**—Travelers 62+ and companions of any age get 10% off all fares. Senior Travel Pak coupons cost $548 for books of four, each good for one leg of domestic flight, including Puerto Rico—a round-trip cost of $274 between TWA cities. A fifth bonus coupon entitles traveler to buy one round-trip ticket to Europe at 20% off any fare.

✓ **A companion of any age traveling with you can buy an additional Travel Pak, including the 20%-off Europe bonus coupon, <u>for the same prices.</u>**

You have a year to redeem coupons for tickets, and another year to travel. You may travel anytime except Sunday noon-to-7 p.m. Make reservations 14 days in advance; stand-bys are permitted. 800/221-2000.

• **United Air Lines**—Travelers 62+ and companions get 10% discounts on published fares; club membership is no longer required. Silverpack Coupons for fliers 62+

but not their companions, with no restrictions on days of travel or blackout dates, cost $596 for four. Two coupons are required to fly one-way to Hawaii and Alaska. The exception: It takes only one coupon to fly between Seattle and Anchorage or Fairbanks. You have a year to redeem coupons, another year to travel. You may travel any day. Make reservations 14 days in advance, but stand-bys are permitted. 800/241-6522.

Silver Wings Plus Travel Club for travelers 55+ costs $75 for two years, $150 for lifetime membership, but fees are credited toward ticket purchases. Companions of any age may join, provided they fly with you. Members get travel packages, hotel, car-rental and other discounts. Members 62+ also get 10% discounts on United flights, but partner deals offering seniors lower fares on some international airlines have been discontinued. To join, call 214/760-0022.

- **United Shuttle**—Since October 1994 this new airline has scheduled frequent flights between major cities at fares lower than major airlines'. Travelers 62+ get 10% discounts on all fares, and those 65+ get even lower discounts, varying by destinations. Example: regular $69 one-way flight between Los Angeles and San Francisco costs fliers 62+ $62. Passengers 65+ pay only $57. 800/748-8853.

- **USAir**—Travelers 62+ and their younger companions get 10% discounts on posted fares. A Golden Opportunities coupon for those 62+ is good for one leg of travel anywhere on USAir's domestic system, including Puerto Rico and St. Thomas. Coupons cost $596 for four—$298 a round-trip.

✓ **Your grandchildren 2-11 can fly on your coupons—you don't have to buy separate books for them. Thus, you could visit San Juan with a grandchild for $271 each—little more than half the best fare we know of.**

Travel is permitted any time, with no blackout dates. You have to fly within one year of purchasing the coupons, and you need 14-day advance reservations; stand-bys are allowed. 800/428-4322.

- **USAir Shuttle**—Travelers 62+ pay half-fare—$146 for round trips vs. $292 regular fare—between Boston-

Airline Deals

New York or New York-Washington. You have to fly between 10 a.m. and 2 p.m. weekdays, after 7 p.m. or on Saturdays or Sundays. No senior-discount coupon books. 800/428-4322. ❐

Savings When You Fly The Internet

Almost all the airlines now have home pages on the World Wide Web. Some are experimenting with the Web as a new way to sell tickets. Mature travelers who are comfortable going on-line should be alert for airfare bargains at these Web sites.

American Airlines has been using the internet to sell advance-purchase coach tickets that didn't sell in advance, producing bargains for nimble travelers of half off or more. Example: A Chicago-L.A. round-trip ticket, ordinarily $331, recently sold for $169.

About 60,000 are signed up for the e-mail service, AA says. Sign-up is free; just get to American Airlines' home page on the web: http://www.amrcorp.com. Check the "NetSAAver Fares" entries. Every Wednesday you'll get an e-mail on last-minute fare offers for the next weekend. You sign up right on the net. You have to use the bargain tickets the following Saturday, and return on Monday or Tuesday.

Similar deals are USAir's E-Saver Discounts ast http://www.usair.com, and Northwest Airlines' CyberSavers at http://www/nwa.com.

American also tinkered with a ticket auction on its web site which produced even deeper savings—maybe too low, because American's ticket-auction operation right now is in limbo.

Happy surfing, seniors!

International Airfare Discounts

Here are airline discounts for seniors on international flights:

Airline	Discount	Age	Comp. Fare	Phone
Aerolineas Arg'ntinas	10%	60+	No	800/333-0276
Aeromexico	10%	62+	No	800/237-6639
Air Canada	10%	60+	Yes	800/776-3000
Air France	10%	62+	No	800/237-2747
Air New Zealand	10%	55+	No	800/262-1234
Alitalia	10%	62+	Yes	800/223-5730
America West	10%	62+	Yes	800/235-9292
British Airways	10%	60+	Yes	800/247-9297
BWIA International	10%	62+	Yes	800/327-7401
Cayman Airways	10%	62+	Yes	800/441-3003
Continental*	10%	62+	Yes	800/231-0856
Delta	10%	62+	Yes	800/241-4141
El Al Israel Airline	15%	60+	55+	800/223-6700
Finnair	10%	62+	Yes	800/950-5000
Hawaiian Air	10%	60+	No	800/367-5320
Iberia Airlines	10%	62+	No	800/772-4642
KLM Royal Dutch	10+%**	62+	Yes	800/374-7747
Lacsa Airlines	10%	63+	No	800/225-2272
Lufthansa	10%	60+	Yes	800/645-3880
Mexicana	10%	62+	Yes	800/531-7921
Northwest Airlines	10%	62+	Yes	800/225-2525
Sabena	10%	60+	Yes	800/955-2000
SAS	10%	62+	No	800/221-2350
SwissAir	10%	62+	Yes	800/221-4750
TAP Air Portugal	10%	62+	Yes	800/221-7370
TWA	10%	62+	Yes	800/221-2000
United Air Lines	10%	62+	Yes	800/538-2929
USAir	10%	62+	Yes	800/622-1015
Varig	10%	62+	No	800/468-2744
Virgin Atlantic	10%	60+	Yes	800/862-8621

* Continental also offers Golden Global Passports to fliers 62+ (see Continental domestic listing).
** KLM currently offers 30% senior discounts to France.

4. Cruising Along At a Discount

With cruiselines in the midst of rampant discounting, mature travelers need never pay the advertised fare.

For 49ers-plus, cruising can be about the best travel value around.

Cruise fares are tumbling at an astonishing rate. Each year, world-wide, more people take to cruising, and each year a dozen or more new ships come on-line. Many are mega-ships, carrying 1,800, 1,900, 2,000 passengers. By 1998, a 2,600-passenger cruiseship is scheduled for launching. Despite this surge in cruising's popularity, there are still more cabins than people to fill them.

The Low Cost of Cruising

In the cruise business, any fare that works out to be less than $150 a day per person is a true bargain. But often you can cruise the Caribbean, to Mexico and even to Alaska for little more than $100 a day, sometimes less—and that can include airfare!

Nobody is buying cruises at posted prices, according to the authoritative travel-trade publication, *Travel Weekly*.

While posted fares have remained reasonably steady, cruise discounts come in lots of disguises:

If you book your cruise early—say, three months or more, almost all cruiselines offer a few hundred dollars off the price. If you book late, last-minute travel agencies will find you a cut-rate deal on the cruise you want. If you book in-between, cruise-discount agencies will help you out.

In addition, cruise lines unwilling to admit they give discounts will throw in extras: free or low-cost air supplements, free hotel rooms a day or two before or after your cruise, stateroom upgrades, spending certificates to use aboard ship and the like. Some have stretched their cruises—eight days for the price of seven, for example, or Glacier Bay cruises that now go beyond Anchorage. And some operators, like Holland America and Princess Tours, add a land package to their Anchorage cruises—train trips past Mt. McKinley to Fairbanks.

Shop the travel section of your Sunday newspaper for these cruise deals. Try to catch the flavor of the ads. Most cruiselines forbid discounters from advertising in terms of dollars. Look for catchwords like "group discount," or for discounts stated as percentages off regular rates, rather than dollars off.

Because of the bewildering number of cruise deals, you should work through a travel agent to find the best values for the place you want to cruise to. There are retail travel agents, as well as discounters, who specialize just in cruises.

Never pay the advertised price for a cruise unless there are offsetting extras.

Deals at Sea for 49ers+

Because of the rampant discounting and because most cruise passengers are 49ers-plus, senior citizen discounts are rare at sea. Most of those offered are either short-term or one-time deals. But when they are offered, they are very special.

Grand Circle Travel, arranging trips exclusively for 49ers+, was able to cut its Alaska cruise costs in half—a week-long cruise for only $879 a person, a 12-day cruise for $1,379—during the summer of 1996 when it bailed out a cruiseline that had just bought two new cruiseships and had no passen-

Cruising Along

gers to fill the cabins.

Club Med 2 posted a short-term deal for senior couples: a percentage off the cruise fare to French Polynesia based on years of marriage. Those married 40 years got 40% off, half-century couples got 50% off, and so on.

Mature travelers on group tours like Grand Circle Travel's and Ballroom Dancers Without Partners got 25% off fares for inaugural cruises of the mega-liner Sun Princess.

The champions of short-term deals for mature travelers are cruise discounters like The Cruise Line, Inc., of Miami, whose recent discount fares for 49ers+ included a week-long Caribbean cruise for $599 (vs. a posted fare of $1,499), a four-day Baja cruise at $279 (vs. a posted fare of $679). Third and fourth seniors sharing a cabin paid just $99 each!

Unlike these short-term deals at sea, posted senior discounts are more common on the world's inland waters: the Rhine and Europe's canals, the waterways of Russia, Alaska's Marine Highway and the like. Tour packagers such as Mature Tours (800/266-1566) and Canada's I'm Proud To Be Me Travel (800/668-9125 from Canada; 416/447-7683 from the U.S.) offer regular steamboatin' trips on the Mississippi and its tributaries at rates 25%-to-30% below Delta Queen Steamboat Co.'s posted fares.

How to Find the Discounts

Most senior discounts at sea are not advertised. The few that are advertised, mostly in Sunday travel sections of major metropolitan newspapers, do not name the specific cruise, only the agency. To keep posted on these deals, most of which are offered only for a short time, mature travelers can:

- **Sign up with a cruise specialist** that will

notify customers quickly of new discounts that become available.

There are large cruise specialists like The Cruise Line in every major city. They get huge discounts from the cruiselines thanks to the volume of their bookings. But, usually, the agencies can't advertise the discounts. Instead, they're allowed to offer the discounts to their preferred customers through newsletters, fax hotlines or direct contact.

One of the biggest cruise discounters operates out of the Miami area: The Cruise Line, Inc. Its free *World of Cruising Magazine* regularly lists discounts for 49ers+. The Cruise Line puts out hot-sheets on last-minute deals for seniors. To get on that agency's mailing list for senior deals, write 150 N.W. 168th St., North Miami Beach, FL 33169; call 800/327-3021. The agency also maintains a free telephone hotline for solo travelers; to sign up call 800/777-0707, ext. 613.

Another last-minute cruise specialist offering deep discounts is Vacations to Go (800/338-4962), which sends those who sign up a twice-monthly mailing of cruise deals.

• **Subscribe to a periodical** like <u>The Mature Traveler</u>, which regularly lists new and current cruise discounts for seniors, or look for them under "Current Bargain" headings in major Sunday travel sections like *The New York Times*, the *Miami Herald* or *The Los Angeles Times*.

Glossy magazines and books, with long production lead times, cannot guarantee listed deals are still being offered. Even The *Book of Deals* lists discounts only as recent examples, with no guarantees they'll still be around when you call.

Only newsletters and magazines, with production lead times of two weeks or less, can publish up-to-date cruise bargains. For a year's subscription to <u>The Mature Traveler</u>, send $29.95 to P.O. Box 50400, Reno, NV 89513-0400. A subscription form is at the end of this book.

• **Join a last-minute travel club.**

Cruising Along 51

Almost every major city has such club that offers members tours as well as cruises on short notice. About the largest is CUC Travel Services (800/255-0200), with regional hot lines around North America. A three-month trial membership costs $1; annual dues are $49 a year. Others include Worldwide Discount Travel Club of Miami Beach, Fla. (303/534-2082), whose annual dues are $50; and South Florida Cruises of Fort Lauderdale, Fla. (800/327-7447), with no dues.

Positioning Cruises

There are some other cruise bargains that only your travel agent—or maybe your Sunday travel section—can let you in on.

Positioning cruises are one-shot voyages designed to get a ship from a previous home port to a new one. For example, a Vancouver-based ship that sails weekly to Glacier Bay in the summer, will be re-positioned to Miami for weekly Caribbean cruises in winter. Transatlantic positioning cruises through the Panama Canal are also common.

Positioning cruises are a time for crew rotation, for chefs to experiment with new menu items, for lounge entertainers to try out new numbers. Everything takes on a freshness during such a voyage—and there can also be enormous glitches.

The cost will be one-half to two-thirds of what you'd normally pay for such a cruise. Example: when Royal Cruise Lines repositioned Crown Odyssey from San Juan, P.R., to Lisbon, you could have gotten on the 13-day cruise for as little as $1,400 (with an early-booking discount)—and that included round-trip airfare to U.S. gateways and three nights at a Lisbon hotel.

These rates are cheap because cruiselines don't put a lot of advertising or promotion effort into positioning cruises, and yet there have to be passengers to make the cruise work. The cruises are great for retirees, who have the time to take a longer cruise and the flexibility to plan well in advance.

Usually, your travel agent knows when positioning cruises are scheduled, and which ones offer deeply discounted early-booking rates. Just tell your agent you're in the market for such a cruise, and to alert you whenever a good one comes up on the computer.

Gentleman Hosts

Men 45+ who enjoy lots of dancing can cruise almost free by enrolling as gentleman hosts.

Royal Cruise Lines (RCL) pioneered the host programs after marketing studies showed that many more mature women than men cruised alone or in pairs. And many of the women complained there weren't enough dancing partners.

It became the gentleman hosts' assignment to graciously ask any single women to dance, without playing favorites, as long as the band was playing. While hosts were not permitted to make attachments—either on ship or after the cruise—there was always a gentleman to hold a lady's arm when the ship's photographer came around, to assist her on shore trips and make conversation while the band was taking a break. Since then, every cruiseline that has installed a gentleman-host program has been overwhelmed with compliments.

This job takes stamina. Hosts must be able to dance almost every dance into the wee hours, then be up early to escort single ladies on shore trips, chat with them, pose with them for photos, serve as bridge partners (or Scrabble, or hearts, or whatever), help the ship's entertainment crew and, generally, leap over tall smoke stacks, when required.

Despite the "work," these guys seem to have a great time.

At least seven cruiselines have gentleman-host programs on board 20 or more ships; one travel packager also brings gentlemen hosts on its dance cruises. The cruiselines vary the number of hosts on each cruise, depending on passenger mix. Announcing its new program, Cunard said there would be 10 hosts aboard world cruises of QE2 and four aboard Sagafjord world cruises. On regular cruises, QE2, carries four hosts, and Sagafjord and Vistafjord two each.

Cruising Along 53

To qualify as hosts, usually men must be single, widowed or divorced, 45-to-70 years old and good dancers. Except on long cruises, men pay their own airfare to the ship. The cruiseline provides the men free passage, free shore excursions and often a bar tab to pay for the women's drinks.

The leading agency recruiting gentleman hosts, Lauretta Blake's The Working Vacation, sends potential hosts applications, then visits them for dance reviews and personal interviews. Once selected, the gentleman pays the Blake agency a placement fee plus $150 a week for every week he's on cruise—the cruiselines don't get the money.

As for dress, Blake requires men to own a tux (except those aboard the less-formal Mississippi Queen and American Queen), and "strongly suggests that hosts also bring navy blazers, white slacks and white leather shoes for dancing," according to a Blake spokesman, who adds:

"The best gentleman hosts have vivacious energy, sparkling personalities; they are good listeners and pleasant conversationalists. And above all, they must love to dance."

Blake handles gentleman host programs for Holland America, Delta Queen Steamboat Co., Cunard (including former Royal Viking Line ships), Orient Lines, Silver Sea and World Explorer Alaska and Caribbean cruises. Contact Lauretta Blake's The Working Vacation, 610 Pine Grove Court, New Lenox, IL 60451; call 815/485-8307.

There is no fee to try out as a gentleman host on Crystal Cruises' upscale ships, Harmony and Symphony. For an application form, write Peter Johnson or Kirk Frederick, Crystal Cruises Entertainment Dept. (Guest Programs), 2121 Avenue of the Stars, Los Angeles, CA 900676. Don't phone.

Merry Widows, a Tampa, Fla., tour packager that brings its own gentleman hosts along on cruises and other dancing trips for women traveling solo, also does not charge a fee. Write Phyllis W. Zeno, Director, Merry Widows, 1515 N. Westshore Blvd., Tampa, FL 33607. ❑

Cruise Deals For Mature Travelers

Here are age-based cruise discounts around the world. Mature travelers can book most of these deals through their travel agent or a cruise discounter.

Alaska—Passengers 65+ get half-off fares between all Alaska ports on Alaska Marine Highway ferries Oct. 1-April 30. Passage for seniors is just $5 between some ports all year. Call 800/642-0066.

Caribbean: Passengers 65+ and cabin-mates of any age get 10%-to-15% off fares on Premier Cruise Lines Bahamas cruises from east Florida ports. In the fall, discounts for mature travelers often are deeper. 800/327-7113 . . . Costa Cruises gives passengers 60+ 10% discounts on tickets purchased at least 90 days before the cruise. 800/327-2537 . . . Passengers 55+ get 10% discounts on week-long voyages of the tall ship Sir Francis Drake through the British Virgin Islands that regularly cost $895-$995. Deal is good through June 1997. 800/662-0090.

France—49ers+ get 15% discounts on barge trips throughout France, Belgium and Holland. Call Lanikai Cruises, 800/487-6630.

Hawaii—Passengers 55+ get 15% off Royal Hawaiian Cruises' day-trips through the islands that range from $45 to $135. 800/852-4183.

Norway—Those 67+ get $100 off round-trip fares, $50 off one-way fares, on Bergen Line coastal ferries all year except June and July. 800/323-7436 . . . Silja Line and other Scandinavian ferry lines also give seniors various discounts on Baltic cruises. Book through your travel agent.

Russia—Travelers 55+ get 10%-20% discounts on riverboat cruises on selected sailing dates from Value World Tours—savings of $500-$800 a person. 800-795-1633 . . . Unique World Travel gives travelers 55+ $100 off Russian and European cruises that regularly start at $1,699. 800/669-0757.

5. Auto Rental Offers You <u>Can</u> Refuse

Shoppers, not AARP or Mature Outlook members, still get the best deals in this chaotic business.

A long-running travel myth is the auto-rental discounts that major senior organizations such as Mature Outlook, AARP and CARP offer their members.

Auto-rental rates are chaotic, with some of the best discounts often available to travelers of all ages. In its regular surveys, *The Mature Traveler* finds that seniors are sometimes quoted higher rates than younger travelers. The reason is that senior discounts are taken off the full, posted rental rate of the car. Auto agencies' "promotional rates"—that is, local sale prices—almost always are lower, sometimes up to half off.

The truth is that the people who get real car-rental bargains are travelers of any age who shop hard and bargain best.

Car-rental agencies don't make shopping easy, either: The rate quoted will never be the rate you drive out with, thanks to state and local taxes, airport fees imposed on off-airport car-rental offices and other tarrifs that the 800-toll-free reservation desks won't or can't tell you. These can add up to 26% to the rental rate quoted, according to a survey by Travel Industry Association of America (TIA).

Be wary, also, of other hidden charges, like

insurance coverage, called CDW for "collision damage waver," mileage limits and extra fuel charges. A new ploy is an option that lets you buy a tank of gas when you start, then bring back the car empty of fuel "without penalty." You'll be told that option lets you avoid having to hunt for a filling station on your way back to the rental office.

The truth is that nobody can bring the car back perfectly empty. If you leave a quarter tank, you will have have bought the rental company two or three gallons of gas—and paid a premium for the privilege!

A $64 Saving for Half-an-Hour's Shopping

Headed for his 40th-anniversary high-school class reunion, Jason Rhoades of Los Angeles recently shopped for a compact rental car to use on a four-day weekend in Kansas City.

"I hung on the phone for maybe a half-hour," says Rhoades, "and saved almost $64." Here's how:

He used toll-free 800-numbers to call nationwide car-rental firms with offices in Kansas City, bargained hard and asked for his senior discounts.

Rhoades says the actual drive-out rates he negotiated varied from $16.19 a day (Thrifty Car Rental) to a high of $31.92 (Alamo)—almost double. Ironically, neither of these companies gives an AARP discount; the lowest AARP rate Rhoades was able to negotiate was $19.02 a day with National Car Rental.

To illustrate the hidden costs, the lowest drive-out rate was based on a quoted weekend rate of $15.89, less a 10% senior discount—a total of $14.30—plus 13.225% in sales taxes and off-airport fees.

To illustrate the chaos in the business, the quoted rate actually fell 50¢—from $16.39 to $15.89—while Rhoades was on the phone with Thrifty!

All seven car-rental companies contacted were able to quote Kansas City's 6.225% sales tax as an add-on to the base rate—once Rhoades pressed about any extras. Thrifty's national reservation desk also knew about Kansas City's 7% "airport

Car Rentals

access tax," levied on rental agencies that collect you at the airport and drive you to off-airport offices.

Rule-of-Thumb: Pay $25 a Day

As a generalization, _TMT's_ surveys have shown for a number of years that Thrifty offers the lowest rates, as well as the most honest senior discounts—a guaranteed 10% off the lowest posted rates.

Hertz is almost always the highest for a particular location, and Alamo's rates the most erratic.

Usually, you'll pay a higher day-rate than Rhoades negotiated for a weekend in Kansas City. Weekday rates are at least 50% higher, sometimes nearly double those on weekends. Rhoades tells of one reservations spokesman who said his company's rate was low because it was a "low-demand period."

"In other words, there were no regular rates—only what the market would bear," says Rhoades.

We have been quoted—but never paid—up to $50 a day for a compact. We are usually satisfied—and stop shopping—when we' have negotiated a weekday rate of $25 or less.

Rhoades says his AARP and Mature Outlook memberships didn't count for much—his AAA membership got him about the same discount.

Before you're tempted to drop your AARP membership, though, remember that most rent-a-car companies giving genuine senior-citizen bargains give them just to AARP, CARP or Mature Outlook members—not to all seniors. Thrifty is an exception.

How to Shop for a Car Rental

Chances are your travel agent can shop for you. Just tell the agent what kind of car you want ("compact," "smallest available," "roomy," "cheapest they've got," and so on), what groups you belong to that may have negotiated discounts (Mature Outlook, AARP, AAA, Lions Club, Elks, whatever) and how long you plan to keep the car.

If you do you own shopping, use toll-free 800-numbers and ask for the best drive-out rate—not just the quoted rate—for the car you want on the day you pick it up. Here are more tips for getting the best rate:

- **Check for the senior discount**, and tell the clerk what other groups you belong to that might bring larger discounts—AAA, Hilton HHonors, Gold Card memberships, airline VIP clubs and the like.
- **Ask about extra charges**—sales taxes, state surcharges, airport-access fees and airport-use fees.TIA says these fees can boost actual drive-out rates by 26% in Phoenix, 23% in Tampa, 21% in Las Vegas and New Orleans, 21% in Orlando. *Consumer Reports Travel Letter* ($39 a year, CRTL, P.O. Box 53629, Boulder, CO 80322-3629) suggests you can avoid airport-access fees, which can boost drive-out rates by 10%, by asking the rental company if you can take a shuttle to your hotel and rent from there.
- **Ask about other hidden charges.** If you don't select the rental company's insurance coverages, will there be a credit block? In Florida, some rent-a-car companies put a $3,000 credit hold on your bank card—that is $3,000 you can't use to pay restaurant or hotel bills—until you return the car.
- **Is mileage unlimited?** If you have to pay something like 30¢ a mile over 100 miles, add the extra charge into your price comparisons or you'll be weighing apples and oranges.
- **What is the cost of a second driver?** If it's a dollar or two a day, it's probably worth that much to have a helper when you get tired. If it's $5 or $10 a day, call another rent-a-car company or get by without extra driving help.

There are other ways to save on auto rental if your travel plans are flexible:

- **Avoid high-demand times.** In most cities, you'll get a cheaper rate on weekends than weekdays. Don't expect to get a car at a reasonable rate during Comdex Week in Las Vegas, for example, or during Mardi Gras in New Orleans.

- **Make travel plans as far in advance as possible**, and come up with firm dates. Car-rental rates change daily, depending on demand. Once you have reserved a car and gotten a confirmation number, the rate is guaranteed. It cannot go up—but it can go down.

Always Have a Reservation

Always arrive at your destination with a rental car reservation—if cars are scarce and you can't get one on short notice, it could ruin a trip.

Even when you have a reservation, once your plane lands, call the local rental office from the airport and ask for the best available rate in the next half-hour? Go through the litany of discounts you're eligible for one more time.

If you're quoted a lower rate than the one the national reservation desk quoted you, go for it. Be sure to get the name of the clerk you're talking to; be sure the lower rate you're quoted is guaranteed. And only after you're satisfied you have a deal, tell the clerk:

"By the way, cancel my previous reservation." ❏

Auto Rental Deals for 49ers+

Here are senior-citizen discounts offered by nationwide auto rental companies. The "Sample Cost" column is based on the actual per-day "drive-out" cost of a compact car for a weekend in a sample city, Kansas City, Mo.

Agency	Phone	Senior Deals	Sample Cost
Alamo	800/327-9633	No nationwide senior discount, but may offer deals at some local offices.	$ 31.92
Avis	800/331-1212	15% discounts off full rates to AARP members, 10-15% off to members of other groups.	$ 19.32
Budget	800/527-0700	No nationwide senior discounts; some local offices give seniors up to 10% off full rates.	$ 21.03
Dollar	800/800-4000	No senior discounts.	$ 19.11
Hertz	800/654-3131	13% off full rates to members of senior groups.	$ 24.83
National	800/227-7368	10% off full rates to members of senior groups.	$ 19.02
✓ **Thrifty**	**800/367-2277**	**Guarantees 10% off any published rate to travelers 55+.**	**$ 16.19**
Ent'prise	800/325-8007	10% off full rates to members of senior groups.	$ 30.56
Value	800/327-2501	5% off full rates to travelers 50+	(No K.C. office)
Payless	800/237-2804	Free "Nifty Fifty Club" earns members 50+ $3 off daily rates, $10 off weekly rates.	$ 31.62

6. Great Trains, Great Memories

For mature travelers, a train can be a time machine—a journey into the not-too-distant past.

It's not so important where you go on a train—it's how you get there that's the joy.

Before airlines came along and almost put them out of business, passenger trains were the civilized way to travel from city to city in North America. Now Amtrak and its Canadian counterpart, Via Rail, are trying to restore the ambience of those great trains, with their elegant diners and club cars and superb service.

Instead of vehicles for transportation, North America's trains today are land cruisers—for mature travelers, time machines: journeys into the not-too-distant past.

In contrast, the great trains of Europe never went away; they just got better—almost exotic: Travel from London to Paris beneath the English Channel. Travel across France on a train that goes as fast as some airplanes. Travel from the North Cape to the heel of Italy on a single railpass. See the English countryside from a restored 1930s art deco dining car.

Mature travelers can ride all of these great trains—and get senior discounts, to boot!

Amtrak

Mature travelers can spend weeks aboard the train seeing different parts of America—and at a cost, less than $322, the airlines couldn't begin to match. Amtrak, clearly, wants to have mature travelers' loyalty and business:

For snowbirds who don't look forward to a long

drive, Amtrak runs auto trains between Virginia and Florida. Starting to catch up with the Europeans in speed and service, Amtrak is rolling out high-tech, high-speed trains—trying them out on popular day-excursions between cities like Seattle-Vancouver, B.C., and Los Angeles-Las Vegas.

Amtrak runs trains like the Coast Starlight from Seattle to Los Angeles and the California Zephyr along the old Union Pacific route between Chicago and San Francisco that are truly land cruises, with some of the best mountainscapes in America that you simply can't see from an auto.

From point-to-point, travel on the Amtrak costs about half as much as by air. Amtrak has a complicated fare structure, including a 15% discount for passengers 62+ on coach fares and seasonal specials. But the bargains are All Aboard America Fares that are far below most of Amtrak's other promotional fares. Here's how the passes work:

The country is divided into three regions—East, Midwest (starting at Indianapolis and New Orleans) and West (starting at Denver, Albuquerque and El Paso). You can visit within one region for $288 ($245 for seniors), two regions for $318 ($270 for seniors) and three regions for $378 ($322). You can take 45 days to make your trip, and stop off to visit any three cities along your route.

For $322, you could start out in Boston, for example, and travel to Chicago; change trains for the Twin Cities and Seattle; take the Coast Starlight down through San Francisco to Los Angeles; change again for Phoenix, San Antonio, Houston and New Orleans; and travel back up through Dixie to Washington and home through the Northeast Corridor to Boston. And you could lay over at any three stops along your route, perhaps even taking one of Amtrak's escorted tour packages.

Get information on Amtrak tours, fares and

timetables at any Amtrak station, from your travel agent or from Amtrak Distribution Center, P.O. Box 7717, Itasca, IL 60143 (800/872-7245).

Canada's Via Rail

Mature travelers on Via Rail can take the continent's longest rail trip—3,639 miles between Vancouver and Halifax—and return for less than $380 (U.S.), about the same as the Amtrak fare.

Via Rail gives travelers 60+ 10% off on almost all fares, including its premium Silver & Blue service between Vancouver and Toronto. Traveling on a $421 (U.S.) Canrail Pass ($379 for seniors), passengers can take the trains anywhere in Canada for any 12 days in a 30-day period—time enough for the six-day journey across the continent, then back. Using the pass permits passengers unlimited layovers within those 30 days.

The pricey Silver & Blue service, which includes on-board, sit-down dining and sleepers, costs seniors $1,533 (U.S.). For information, rates, timetables, tours and route maps, call Via Rail at 800/561-3949 (from the U.S.) or 800/561-8630 (from Canada).

Britrail

Considering the country's top-notch rail system, the Senior Flexipass along with its mates, the BritRail Senior Classic Pass and the BritRail Senior Railcard, represent the best way for travelers 60+ to see Great Britain.

Virtually every town in Britain can be reached by train. Departures from larger cities often are only minutes apart, while trains stop at even the smallest villages several times a day.

Here's how the senior passes work:

• **The BritRail Senior Flexipass** lets holders travel in first-class cars on any day and at any time within a certain time period. There are three options: Travel any four days within a month for $245 (younger travelers pay a regular price of $289); travel any eight days within the month for $339 (regularly $399); or travel any 15 days within the month for $490 (regularly $615)—at 20% off, the best senior discount BritRail offers to travelers from North America.

- **The BritRail Senior Classic Pass**, which costs less, requires holders to travel on consecutive days—but they may hop on and off trains as often as they like on those days. An eight-day pass on first-class costs travelers 60+ $275, a 15-day pass $445, a 22-day pass $565 and a 30-day pass $650—15% discounts from rates charged younger passengers.

You have to purchase both BritRail Senior Flexipass and BritRail Senior Classic Pass <u>before</u> you leave home in the United States or Canada.

- **The BritRail Senior Railcard** gives holders 60+ one-third off fares throughout the United Kingdom—the best senior discounts of all. But it is useful mostly to U.K. residents and travelers who plan to stay awhile. You must buy the pass in the U.K. at a cost of £16 and wait 21 days for its delivery.

There are a few rail journeys in Great Britain which do not allow use of BritRail Passes: special excursion trains like the Royal Scotsman that include meals, hotels and the like; the Orient Express and its day-trains in England; and charter trains not listed on regular timetables. BritRail Passes are not accepted in Ireland, nor on the Eurostar, which travels through the Channel Tunnel between London, Paris and Brussels. Eurostar has its own senior discounts.

Get information and buy BritRail Passes from your travel agent or BritRail Travel International (800/677-8585).

Eurotrains

Though individual European countries' rail systems have senior citizen passes or discounts off regular fares, most American travelers in Europe are better off with a EurailPass or a ScanrailPass. After you buy one of these, you can travel free for a fixed period of time anywhere in Western Europe, except Great Britain.

Travelers 60+ also get passage on Eurostar trains, connecting London through the Channel

Great Trains

Tunnel with Brussels and Paris, for 20% off the adult ticket price.

You'll save the most money on a rail pass if you're traveling frequently in several countries, especially the high-fare countries of northern Europe. If you're traveling only in one or two countries, check out other passes and senior discounts offered by their national rail systems. You have to buy these at the station—your travel agent can't help you. If you're planning an extended stay—more than three months—the individual passes with their senior discounts are also better deals.

EurailPasses do the same thing for budget-minded rail travelers on the continent that BritRail Passes do in the U.K. There are seven versions; a EurailPass that lets you ride the trains anywhere in Western Europe for 10 days in 60, for example, costs $616. The version you buy depends on the number of days you want to use the EurailPass, the number of countries you want to use it in, or whether you want a car for a few days. But there is no version for mature travelers.

Scanrail, however, offers mature travelers the Scanrail 55+ Pass, costing about 13% less than a regular Scanrail Pass. With a pass, visitors 55+ can travel on any scheduled train in Denmark, Finland, Norway and Sweden for any four days in a 15-day period. The pass is also good for discounts on ferries ranging from free to 25% off and 10-to-30% discounts off posted hotel rates. Current costs are $193 (vs. regular rate of $222) for a first-class pass, $153 (vs. $176) for second class.

The EurailPass and its derivatives are just for foreign tourists—they're not sold in Europe. Buy them in the United States and Canada from your travel agent or from Rail Europe, 800/438-7245. Write for the free timetable, *Through Europe by Train*, a Eurail map and brochure to CIT Tours, 666 Fifth Ave., New York, NY 10103. ❐

Best Rail Deals For Mature Travelers

Here is a summary of the best discounts for mature travelers on trains around the world—including some excursion trains:

✓ *indicates best values for mature travelers.*

In the United States

Alaska—Travelers 65+ get 25% off fares on Alaska Railroad mid-September to mid-May. 800/544-0552 for reservations.

✓ Amtrak—Travelers 62+ get 15% off lowest coach fares, including All-Aboard America Passes, regularly $278 to cross America. Call 800/872-7245.

Arizona—Clarkdale: Travelers 65+ get $4 off $34.95 fare on Verde Canyon Railroad through Sycamore Canyon. 602/639-0010.

In Canada

British Columbia—49ers+ get 15% off $42 round-trip fare on the Mt. Baker International, new, high-tech excursion train between Seattle and Vancouver. Call 800-872-7245.

Ontario—Ontario Northland gives travelers 60+ 25% off excursion railtour fares through the north country, including Polar Bear Express, from June until Labor Day, and on regular Toronto-Cochrane fares. Call 416/314-3750 (in Canada, 800/268-9281).

✓ Via Rail—The national railway, gives travelers 60+ 10%-to-50% off regular fares, and 10% discounts on Canrail Passes, varying by season. 800/561-3949 (800/561-8630 from Canada).

In Europe

Austria—Senior rail pass for men 65+, women 60+,

Great Trains

costs $25, is good for half-price travel anywhere in the country for a year. Buy passes at the station.

Belgium—Golden Rail Passes for travelers 60+ and companions 55+ are good for six free train trips anywhere in the country, cost $43-to-$67. Buy passes at the station . . . *(Also see Chunnel Train listing.)*

Chunnel Train—Passengers 60+ get 20% off first-class tickets, about 14% off second class on Eurostar trains connecting London with Paris and Brussels, via the English Channel Tunnel. 800/387-6782.

Denmark—Travelers 65+ get half-off most days on Danish rail travel. Buy tickets at the station . . . *(Also see Scandinavia listing.)*

Finland—Travelers 65+ get 50% off rail fares. Buy discount tickets at the stations . . . *(Also see Scandinavia listing.)*

✓ **France**—*Carte Vermeil* costs $28 for four trips, $52 for unlimited trips, gives rail travelers 60+, including those on TGV, half-off for a year during off-peak times, 20% off at peak times. Buy the card from your travel agent or at the railroad station in France.

Germany—Bahn Card, costing $149 for first class, $72 for second class, gives men 65+, women 60+, half-price rail travel. Buy at German railway stations.

✓ **Great Britain**—Travelers 60+ get 15-20% discounts on BritRail Senior Flexpasses and BritRail Senior Classic Passes, good for trains anywhere in the U.K. Get passes from your travel agent before you go or from BritRail, 800/677-8585. BritRail Senior Railcard, costing £16, gives holders 60+ one-third off rail fares; you must buy the Senior Railcard in the U.K. . . . *(Also see Chunnel Train listing.)*

Greece—First five railtrips are free, half-price after that, for holders of Hellenic Railways Pass for travelers 60+. Year's pass costs $45-to-$65. Buy them in Greece.

Italy—Women 61+, men 65+ can buy annual *Carta d'Argento* senior passes at the station ($10), get 30% off rail fares.

Luxembourg—Rail travelers 65+ get half-off fares.

Norway—Travelers 67+ get half off rail fares with passes bought at the station . . . *(Also see Scandinavia listing).*

Portugal—Travelers 65+ get 30% off rail fares. Call 212/354-4403.

Scandinavia—Rail travelers 55+ through Denmark, Finland, Norway, Sweden can buy Scanrail 55+ Passes at 12% off posted cost of ScanrailPass. Buy pass before you leave home. Call 212/949-2333.

Sweden—Rail travelers 65+ get 30% to 50% off fares. Get tickets at the station . . . *(Also see Scandinavia listing.)*

Elsewhere Around the World

New Zealand—Travelers 60+ get "Golden Age" discounts of 30% off regular adult rail fares. Buy tickets at the station.

7. Ski Deals: How 49ers+ Can Save Cold Cash

It's as if senior skiers have an extended family wherever they go in North America.

There are almost 300 ski areas in North America—including popular resorts like Stowe Mountain, Vt., Aspen and Vail in Colorado, and Sundance, Utah—where a special welcome mat is out for mature skiers.

These are the ski areas that offer senior lift-ticket and cross-country trail discounts of 50% or more—savings of $20 to $30 a day—special lodging packages and learn-to-ski programs. At many, seniors ski free.

Already, more than 2 million seniors take at least one ski trip each year. As one novice senior skier put it near the end of last season: "Getting up on a lift to the top of a high mountain and taking my time coming down . . . the views . . . this is the most thrilling thing I've ever done.

"I may have wasted the first 63 years of my life before I learned to ski, but I'm sure not going to spoil the rest of it . . . !"

Almost every ski area has courses for beginners—many geared especially for 49ers+. Low-cost Elderhostels, too, offer ski instruction for those 55+—maybe the best way for seniors to learn skiing.

And for mature travelers who already know how to ski, there are national clubs like the 70-Plus Ski Club and the Over The Hill Gang (OTHG), which host year-around trips to leading ski areas.

In the Northeast and Western U.S., where the

snowpack is most reliable and regulars can visit nearby slopes every week, many resorts sponsor social clubs where senior skiers can meet, trade mountain tales and hone their skiing skills—clubs like the Wild Old Bunch at Alta, Utah, and T.G.I.F. ("Thank Goodness I'm Fifty") Club at Attitash Mountain in Vermont. Typically, these clubs offer lessons for beginners, clinics for advanced skiers, morning coffee or continental breakfasts before skiing, and weekly apres ski parties. Most clubs are free—and they encourage drop-ins by visitors.

It's as if senior skiers have a family wherever they go.

70-Plus Ski Club

At almost every resort in North America, travelers over 70 ski free. For that, you can thank the 70-Plus Ski Club and the persistence of its founder, Lloyd Lambert. Even with 9,000 or so members, the club is pretty much Lambert's one-man show. He founded the club in 1968, when he turned 70.

The club has a long schedule of national outings—all to places where members can ski free—plus Argentina and New Zealand, to name a few recent trips. The club also provides members a quarterly newsletter, discounts on car rentals and trip insurance.

The club supports itself with small annual dues and profits from the outings and other perks. It donates season-end surpluses to the U.S. Olympic Ski Team.

Contact the 70-Plus Ski Club at 104 East Side Dr., Ballston Lake, NY 12019; call 518/399-5458.

Over The Hill Gang

The Over The Hill Gang (OTHG), with more than 3,000 members in 14 chapters around the country, works much like the 70-Plus skiers, with a newsletter, perks and outings to places like the Arlberg Alps, the Canadian Rockies and New Zealand. There is also an occasional white-water rafting or other soft-adventure trip in summer. Local chapters supplement these trips with their

Ski Deals

own outings.

Get information from OTHG, 3310 Cedar Heights Dr., Colorado Springs, CO 80904; call 719/685-4656.

Down-Hill Deals

Here is a sampler of events, special discounts and other promotions exclusively for senior skiers that some leading North American ski resorts have offered. Since these programs change dramatically from ski season-to-season (a value-packed, week-long senior-ski program at Aspen, Colo., was cancelled after its first season, for example; another at Northstar-at-Tahoe, Calif., is constantly growing), don't make plans for your ski trip before calling ahead.

Attitish, Vt.—TGIF ("Thank Goodness I'm Fifty") Club stresses socializing, ski-skills improvement. Group meets weekly for skiing, workshops. Cost for the season has been $20. 800/223-7669.

Breckenridge, Colo.—Specialized two-day "50-Plus Seminars" are taught by seniors for seniors of all skiing abilities. Cost of $140 a person, includes lift tickets, lessons, video analysis and a group dinner. There are usually two sessions each season, in January and February. Breckenridge also hosts "Senior Games of the Summit" competition in February. 970/453-3256.

Cranmore, Vt.—"Heritage Program" for senior skiers features three hours of instruction each Friday with veteran skier Herbert Schneider. The program has been priced at $125 for the season. 800/786-6754.

Crystal Mountain, Thompsonville, Mich.—In addition to lift-ticket and cross-country trail discounts, skiers 55+ get 10% off midweek lodging packages. 616/378-2000.

Lookout Pass, Wallace, Idaho—Fridays are "Boomers Days," when skiers 40+ get half-price lift tickets, half off on one-hour lessons (reg. $18) and equipment-rental discounts. On an accompanying deal, for $32 each four senior skiers got Thursday-night lodging and two days of lift tickets. Deals are from Jan. 1 through March 1. 208/556-7211.

Northstar at Tahoe, Calif.—Three three-day "Golden Stars Ski Clinics" for seniors of all skill levels were recently priced at $153 for skiers 60-69, $103 for skiers 70+. Clinics are in December, January and March. One-hour "Ski Improvement Clinics," scheduled every Wednesday except holidays, are free for seniors who hold lift tickets (recently costing $22 for those 60-69, $5 for those 70+). 916/562-2471.

Schweitzer Mountain, Sandpoint, Idaho—"Prime Timers Club" for skiers 55+ hosts a season-long series of events, including a bargain seniors' ski week in March. "The Snowmasters Classic" week March 3-8, costing about $275 a person, includes five nights' lodging, four days' skiing, shopping trips to the nearby town of Sandpoint and a daily menu of other social activities. "Prime Time Socials" for club members every Thursday afternoon features wine tastings, pizza dinners and the like. Prime Timers also act as tour guides and special-events volunteers. 800/831-8810.

Snowbird, Utah—Pro skier Junior Bounous, who has taught skiing for 45 years, hosts weekly sessions for advanced senior skiers. A week-long "Senior Seminar," is often scheduled in February. Recently costing $390 a person, it included four days' ski instruction, daily breakfasts, lectures, demonstations, video analysis and a closing banquet. "Junior's Seniors" are free, two-hour Tuesday morning sessions for skiers 62+; sessions continue Tuesday afternoons for $15 with lectures and instruction by Bounous. "Silver Wings" are Wednesday and Thursday classes for advanced skiers 55+—one day recently cost $58 a person, two days $100. Weekly sessions run from mid-December through mid-April. Call 801/742-2222.

Sun Valley, Idaho--"Prime Time Specials" weeks for skiers 60+, usually in late January, early February, include seven nights' lodging, five days of lift tickets or trail passes and activities like touring, racing and big-band dances. Recent cost was $380--$114 less than comparable packages for younger skiers. 800/634-3347.

Ski Deals

Cross-Country

A growing number of resorts offer cross-country ski discounts to mature travelers, plus packages that include lodging, cut-rate equipment rentals, lessons and trail passes.

Typical is the "Silver Streak" program at Crystal Mountain, Mich. (616/378-2000), where guests 55+ have been offered half-off trail passes, 20% discounts on equipment rental and free lessons. Major cross-country resorts like Cascade Lodge at Lutsen, Minn. (218/387-1112) give guests 60+ 25% off rooms on weeknights.

Cross-country novices 60+ who join the "Silver Striders Golden Gliders" clinics at Lapland Lake (518/863-4974), near Northville, N.Y., get free lessons from fellow seniors, free equipment rental and a trail pass.

Cross-country ski areas offering packages for seniors are listed in *The Best of Cross Country Skiing*, a guide published by the Cross Country Ski Areas Association. For a copy, send $3 to CCSAA, 259 Bolton Rd., Winchester, NH 03471.

Cross-country ski areas currently offering mature travelers discounts are listed at the end of this chapter.

Elderhostel Lessons

If you're not sure you'll enjoy skiing, Elderhosteling is a great way for beginners to find out without taking a week at a costly ski resort or spending a lot on equipment. For more advanced skiers, the low-cost Elderhostel ski sessions are an inexpensive way to get a few days on the slopes or trails and to brush up on skiing technique.

Here are the kinds of things skiers are taught, according to this description of an Elderhostel program on Vancouver Island, B.C.:

"Certified Nordic instructors teach basic cross-country skills for beginners and share with hostelers their love for skiing. Topics covered include equipment choices, snow conditions and corresponding base preparation . . . Program offers two days of instruction. Downhill instructors patiently introduce the sport of Alpine skiing on gentle beginner slopes . . . Equipment use, slope safety and skier etiquette are all covered during these last three days." The whole ski week, including lodging and meals, costs less than $350.

And who could resist the joys of cross-country after reading this lyrical description of an Elderhostel course in northern Minnesota: "Cross-country skiing and snowshoeing in a Minnesota Boreal forest . . . Learn and review skiing and snowshoeing techniques with resident staff on top-rated trails. We guide students of all abilities through groomed wooded trails and across scenic lakes." That program cost under $300 for the week.

What more can a senior skier ask?

More than 60 winter Elderhostel programs offer instruction in both downhill and cross-country skiing. There is at least one Elderhostel skiing program in every Snowbelt state and province from southern Utah to the Arctic Circle. Programs are limited to those 55+, and their companions 50+.

Ski programs are listed in Elderhostel's United States and Canada Winter Catalog, distributed every September. For a copy and an application form, write Elderhostel 75 Federal St., Boston, MA 02110; call 617/426-9056. ❒

Downhill Ski Deals For 49ers+

These North American ski areas offer special discounts for mature travelers, typically 50% or more off for lift tickets for skiers as young as 50.

* Indicates where skiers 70+ ski free.

\# Indicates lodging/ski packages for seniors.

Alaska—#Alpenglow, 907/428-1208; Alyeska, 907/783-2222; #Eaglecrest, 907/586-5284.

Alberta—#Banff Springs, 403/762-2211; Fortress Mountain, 403/245-4909; #Jasper Park, 800/828-7447; #Kananaskis, 403/591-7770; Lake Louise, 403/256-8473; Marmot Basin, 403/852-3861; Nakiska, 403/591-7777; Sky Mystic, 403/762-4421.

Arizona—*Arizona Snowbowl, 520-779-1951; *#Sunrise, 520-735-7600; *Williams, 520-635-9330.

British Columbia—Blackcomb Mountain, 604/932-3141; Whistler Mountain, 604/932-3434.

California—Alpine Meadows, 916/583-4232; *Badger Pass, 209/372-1445; Bear Mountain, 909/866-7000; *Bear Valley, 209/753-2301; *Boreal, 916/426-3668; *#Dodge Ridge, 800/446-1333; Donner Ski Ranch, 916/426-3635; Heavenly, 916/541-7544; Homewood, 916/525-2900; #Iron Mountain, 209/258-4672; Kirkwood, 209/258-6000; Lassen Park, 916/595-3376; Mammoth Mountain, 619/934-2571; Mountain High, 619/249-5801; #Mount Shasta, 916/926-8610; #Northstar, 916/562-1010; #Sierra Summit, 209/893-3305; Sierra Ski Ranch, 916/659-7475; Snow Summit, 909/866-5841; Snow Valley, 909/867-2751; *Soda Springs, 916/426-3668; Squaw Valley, 800/545-4350; Sugar Bowl, 916/426-3847; *Tahoe Donner, 916/587-9444.

Colorado—*Arapahoe, 800/222-0188; *Arrowhead, 800/332-3029; *#Aspen, 800/525-6200; *Aspen Highlands, 800/356-8811; *Beaver Creek, 800/525-2257; *Breckenridge, 800-221-1091; Buttermilk Mountain,

303/925-1221; *Conquistador, 303/873-9294; *Copper Mountain, 800/458-8386; *Crested Butte, 800/544-8448; *Cochura Valley, 800/227-4436; *Eldora Mountain, 303/440-8700; *Howelsen, 303/879-2043; *Keystone, 800/222-0188; *Loveland, 800/225-5683; *Monarch, 719/539-3573; *Powderhorn, 800/241-6997; *#Purgatory, 800/525-0892; *Silver Creek, 800/462-5253; *Ski Cooper, 719/486-3684; *Ski Sunlight, 800/221-0098; *#Snowmass, 800/525-6200; *#Steamboat, 800/922-2722; *Telluride, 800/525-3455; *Vail, 800/622-3131; *Winter Park, 800/453-2525.

Connecticut—#Mohawk Mountain, 203/672-6464; Powder Ridge, 203/349-3454; #Ski Sundown, 860/379-9851.

Idaho—#Bogus Basin, 800/367-4397; *Brundage Mountain, 800/888-7544; *Grand Targhee, 800/827-4433; #Lookout Pass, 208/556-7211; Pebble Creek, 208/775-4452; #Schweitzer, 800/831-8810; Silver Mountain, 208/783-1111; Ski Brundage, 208/634-7462; Soldier Mountain, 208/764-2526; #Sun Valley, 80/634-3347.

Illinois—*Chestnut Mountain, 800/397-1320; #Snowstar, 309/798-2666; Villa Olivia, 708/289-5200.

Indiana—#Perfect North, 812/537-3754; Ski Paoli Peaks, 812/723-4696.

Iowa—*#Sundown 319/556-6676.

Maine—#Lost Valley, 207/784-1561; Moosehead, 800/348-6743; Mount Abram, 207/875-2601; *Saddleback, 207/864-5671; #Shawnee Peak, 207/647-8444; Sugarloaf, 800/843-5623; #Sunday River, 207/824-6400.

Massachusetts—Berkshire East, 413/339-6617; Bosquet, 413/442-8316; #Brodie, 413/443-4752; Butternut Basin, 800/438-7669; *Catamount, 413/528-1262; Jiminy Peak, 413/738-5500; #Mount Tom, 413/536-0416; Nashoba Valley, 508/692-3033; *Otis Ridge, 413/269-4444; #Wachusett, 800/754-1234.

Michigan—Alpine Valley, 810/887-4183; Big Powder, 906/932-4838; #Bittersweet, 616/694-2032; #Blackjack, 906/229-5115; Boyne, 800/462-6963; Caberfae, 800/678-2931; #Crystal Mountain, 616/378-2000; #Grand Traverse, 800/748-0303; Indianhead, 800/346-3426; Mount Brighton, 810/229-9581; Mount Zion, 906/932-3718; *Norway

Ski Deals

Mountain, 414/837-2300; *#Nub's Nob, 616/526-2131; #Shanty Creek, 800/678-4111; Sugar Loaf, 800/968-0576; #Swiss Valley, 616/244-5635; #Timber Ridge, 616/694-9449; Tree/Sylvan, 800/444-6711.

Minnesota—#Giants Ridge, 800/475-7669; #Hyland Hills, 612/835-4604; Powder Ridge, 612/398-7200; *Spirit Mountain, 800/642-6377.

Montana—#Big Mountain, 406/862-1900; Big Sky, 800/548-4486; #Bridger Bowl, 800/223-9609; Great Divide, 406/449-3746; Maverick Mountain, 406/834-3454; #Red Lodge, 406/446-2610; Showdown, 406/236-5522; Snowbowl, 406/549-9777.

Nebraska—#Trailbridge, 402/332-3313.

Nevada—*#Diamond Peak, 702/832-1175; Lee Canyon, 702/646-0008; #Mount Rose, 702/849-0704.

New Hampshire—#Attitash, 603/374-2368; *Balsams, 800/255-0600; *Black Mountain, 603/383-4490; Bretton Woods, 800/232-2972; #Cannon Mountain, 603/823-5563; Cranmore Mountain, 603/356-5544; *#Dartmouth, 603/795-2143; Gunstock, 800/486-7862; *King Pine, 800/373-3754; *#Loon Mountain, 603/745-8111; *McIntyre, 603/624-6571; Mount Sunapee, 603/763-2356; Pat's Peak, 603/428-3245; *Ragged Mountain, 603/768-3475; *Temple Mountain. 603/924-6949; *#Waterville Valley, 800/468-2553; *Whaleback, 603/448-1489; *Wildcat, 800/255-6439.

New Jersey—#Cragmeur, 201/697-4500; Hidden Valley, 201/764-6161.

New Mexico—*Angel Fire, 800/633-7463; Enchanted Forest, 505/754-6112; Pajarito Mountain, 505/662-5725; Red River, 505/754-2223; *Sandia Peak, 505/242-9133; *Santa Fe, 505/982-4429; *Sipapu Lodge, 505/587-2240; Ski Apache, 505/336-4356; *Snow Canyon, 800/333-7542; *Taos Ski Valley, 505/776-2291.

New York—*Belleayre Mountain, 914/254-5600; *Big Tupper, 518/359-7902; Bristol Mountain, 716/374-6000; *#Catamount 518/325-3200; Cockaigne, 716/287-3223; *Dry Hill, 315/782-8584; *#Four Seasons, 315/637-9023; *#Gore Mountain, 518/251-2411; #Greek Peak, 800/955-2754; *Holiday Mountain, 914/796-3161; #Holiday Valley, 716/699-2345; #Hunt Hollow, 716/374-8833; *Hunter Mountain, 518/263-4223; #Kissing Bridge, 716/592-4963; #Labrador Mountain, 607/842-6204; *#Mount Van Hoberg, 518/523-2811; *Oak Mountain, 518/548-7311; #Peak 'N Peek, 716/355-4141; *#Rocking Horse, 914/691-2927; *Shu-Maker Mountain, 315/823-4470; #Ski Windham, 800/729-7549; Snow Ridge, 315/348-8456; Sterling Forest, 914/351-2163; #Swain, 607/545-6511; #Toggenburg, 315/683-5842; *Villa Roma, 315/686-7234; *#Whiteface Mountain, 518/946-2223; #Woods Valley, 315/827-4721.

North Carolina—*Catalooche, 704/926-0285; *Wolf Laurel, 704/689-4111.

Ohio—#Snow Trails, 419/522-7393.

Oregon—*Anthony Lakes, 541/963-4599; *Ashland, 541/482-2897; Hoodoo Bowl, 541/822-3799; #Mount Bachelor, 541/382-2607; #Mount Hood Meadows, 800/929-2754; Mount Hood Ski Bowl, 503/272-3206; *Spout Springs, 541/566-2164; Timberline, 503/231-5404; Willamette Pass, 541/484-5030l.

Pennsylvania—*Big Boulder Lake, 717/443-8425; *Blue Knob, 814/239-5111; Blue Marsh, 215/488-6399; Camelback, 717/629-1661; *#Eagle Rock, 800/338-2180; Hidden Valley, 800/458-0175; *Jack Frost Mountain, 717/443-8425; Ski Roundtop, 717/432-9631.

South Dakota—#Terry Peak, 800/456-0524.

Utah—Alta, 801/742-3333; *Beaver Mountain, 801/753-0921; *Brian Head, 801/677-2035; *Brighton, 801/532-4731; Deer Valley, 801/649-1000; *Elk Meadows, 801/438-5433; Nordic Valley, 801/745-3511; *Park City, 801/649-8111; Powder Mountain, 801/745-3772; Snowbasin, 801/399-1135; *#Snowbird, 801/742-2222; *Solitude, 801/534-1400; *#Sundance, 801/225-4107; *Wolf Mountain, 801/649-5400.

Vermont—*Ascutney Mountain, 802/484-7711; *Bolton Valley, 802/434-2131; *#Bromley, 802/824-5522; Burke Mountain, 802/626-3305; Haystack, 802/464-5321; #Jay Peak, 800/451-4449; Killington, 802/422-3266; Mad River Glen, 802/496-3551; #Magic Mountain, 802/824-5645; *Middlebury, 802/388-4356; Mount Snow, 802/464-3333; #Okemo Mountain, 802/228-4041; *Pico, 802/775-4345; *Smuggler's Notch, 800/451-8752; #Stowe Mountain, 800/247-8693; *#Stratton Mountain, 800/843-6867; *Sugarbush, 800/537-8427; #Suicide Six, 802/457-1622.

Ski Deals

Virginia—Bryce, 540/856-2121; *#Homestead, 540/839-1766; Massanutten, 540/289-9441; *Wintergreen, 800/325-2200.

Washington—Mission Ridge, 509/996-2148; *Mount Baker, 360/734-6771; *Stevens Pass, 206/973-2441; *The Pass, 206/232-8182; White Pass, 509/453-8731.

West Virginia—*#Canaan Valley, 304/866-4121; Silver Creek, 304/572-4000; Snowshoe, 304/572-5252.

Wisconsin—Alpine Valley, 414/642-7374; Cascade Mountain, 800/992-2754; Christie Mountain, 715/868-7869; Mount Ashwabay, 715/779-3227; *#Mount LaCrosse, 800/426-3665; Nordic Mountain, 715/249-5703; #Rib Mountain, 715/845-2846; Skyline, 608/339-3421; #Sunburst, 414/626-8408; Trollhaugen, 715/755-2955; Tyrol Basin, 608/437-4135; #Wintergreen, 608/588-2571; #Christmas Mountain, 608/253-1000.

Wyoming—*#Grand Targhee, 800/827-4433; #Jackson Hole, 800/443-6931; Snow King, 800/522-5464; Teton Village, 307/733-2292.

Yukon Territory—Mount Sima, 403/667-5608.

Cross-Country Ski Deals for 49ers+

Senior-friendly areas that offer mature travelers free or discounted cross-country ski-trail passes, lodging discounts or special instruction include:

Alberta—Jasper Park Lodge, 403/852-3301; Strathcona Wilderness, 403/922-3939.

British Columbia—Silver Star Mountain, 604/542-0224.

California—Montecito-Sequoia Lodge, 800/227-9900; Northstar-at-Tahoe XC, 916/4587-0245; Royal Gorge at Soda Springs, 916/426-3871; Coffee Creek Ranch, 916/266-3343.

Colorado—Breckenridge Nordic Center, 303/453-6855; Eldora Nordic Center, 303/440-8700; Vista Verde Ranch, 303/879-3858.

Connecticut—Winding Trails XC , 203/677-8458.

Idaho—Sun Valley Nordic Center, 208/622-4111.

Maine—Sunday River, 207/824-2410; Troll Valley XC, 207/778-3656.

Massachusetts—Swift River Inn, 413/634-5751; Northfield Mountain, 413/659-3715.

Michigan—Cross Country Ski Headquarters, 517/821-6661; Oakland County Parks & Rec, 313/858-0906; Corsair Ski Trails, 800/558-2927; Crystal Mountain Resort, 616/378-2000; Boyne Nordican XC Center, 616/549-2441; Wilderness Valley, 616/585-7141.

Minnesota—Maplelag at Callaway, 800/322-9543; Cascade Lodge, Lutsen, 800/322-9543.

Montana—Glacier Nordic Center, 800/321-8822; Big Mountain, 800/858-5439.

New Hampshire—Balsams Wilderness, 800/255-0600; Bretton Woods, 603/278-5181; Great Glen Trails, 603/466-2333; Gunstock, 800/486-7862; King Pine, 800/373-3754; Loon Mountain, 603/745-8111 (ext. 5568); Mount Washington Valley, 603/356-9920; Nordic Skier, 603/569-3151; Norsk, 800/426-6775; Temple Mountain, 603/924-6949; Waterville Valley,

Ski Deals

800/468-2553; Windblown, 603/878-2869.

New Mexico—Manzano Mountain, 505/384-2209; Enchanted Forest, 505/754-2374.

New York—Lapland Lake, 518/863-4974; Frost Valley Ski Center, 914/985-2291; Glenns Falls International XC Trails, 518/793-5676; and Garnet Hill, 518/251-2821.

Nova Scotia—Ski Martock near Windsor, 902/798-9501.

Oregon—Summit Ski Area, 503/294-2104; Mount Bachelor Nordic Center, 503/382-2442.

Pennsylvania—Crystal Lake Ski Center, 717/584-2698.

Ontario—Duntroon Highlands, 705/444-5017; Hardwood Hills north of Toronto, 705/487-3775.

Quebec—Hotel L'Esterel, 800/363-3623; Parc Du Mont-Ste-Anne, 418/827-4561; Camp Mercier (Laurentides), 418/848-2422.

Utah—Brian Head, 800/245-3754; Rujby's Inn, 801/834-5341; Solitude (70+), 801/536-5774; Sundance (65+), 801/225-4107; White Pine (65+), 801/649-8701.

Vermont—Lake Morey Inn, 802/333-4311; Grafton Ponds XC Center, 802/843-2400; Blueberry Hill, 802/247-6735; Craftsbury Nordic Ski Center, 802/586-2514; Burke Mountain, 802/626-8828.

West Virginia—Timberline Ski Resort, 304/866-4801.

Wisconsin—Minocqua Winter Park, 715/356-3309.

Wyoming—Grand Targhee Nordic Center, 307/353-2300.

8. How Solo Travelers Beat Those Dreaded Single-Supplements

Seniors who travel alone are penalized most—but here are some ways to help you fight back.

Those who go in pairs almost always travel cheaper than those who go alone. The bugaboo is called the "single supplement." It hits mature travelers hardest because these are the people who most often travel by themselves.

Tour operators usually add hundreds of dollars to what solos pay for a trip because single travelers stay in staterooms or at inns by themselves. At hotels and motels, a person occupying a room alone often pays the same rate as two people occupying the same room—a 100% penalty. Those who cruise alone also pay "single supplement" penalties ranging up to 100%. And despite the higher cost, a solo often winds up in a pie-shaped room behind the elevator, or in a tiny cabin near the galley.

Unfair? Unethical? How can they charge double when one cruiseship passenger eats only half as much as two, and one bed takes only half as long to make as two?

"The economics of meeting the overhead" is the explanation of one cruiseship executive: The show must go on whether it's being watched by one person or two--or 200, for that matter. The ship's crew isn't reduced and the fuel bill is the same no matter how many occupy a cabin. Similarly, at a motel when a solo guest sleeps in one bed and may unpack baggage on the other, both beds have to be made up; all towels have to be replaced; the entire bathroom has to be cleaned.

So the single supplement is likely to stay around. The only sure strategy for avoiding the penalty is to find a traveling companion. But there are other ways for clever solo travelers to hold the costs in check.

Travel Matchmakers

If you can't get Aunt Dorothy or your next-door neighbor to travel with you, you can find a companion through a travel matchmaker club, through a publication or through the tour company's single-share program.

To help you find a companion, there are several travel-matchmaker clubs that operate nationwide, some just for mature travelers.

These clubs charge annual or semi-annual dues, have you fill out a questionnaire (things like your personal habits, travel habits, where you want to go and the like) and publish the information with a code number or pen name in a regular newsletter for members. Then it's up to you to contact other club members you're interested in traveling with.

After that, members often correspond for awhile, talk by phone and even take short trips together to make sure they really are compatible. Many solo travelers belong to more than one club.

Here are the leading travel-matchmaker clubs:

Golden Companions—Membership is limited to solo travelers over 45. The club has about 400 members, and, in addition to benefits like a directory and a regular newsletter, *Golden Gateways*, facilitates tours and other member get-togethers. Annual dues are $94; a six-month introductory membership is $49.95.

Contact Golden Companions, P.O. Box 5249, Reno, NV 89513; call 702/324-2227.

Partners For Travel—Also for travelers over 45, Partners For Travel takes a more active hand in matchmaking by sending new members information about prospective travel partners who seem compatible. Any single, member or not, can participate in the club's singles-only trips. With dues at $60 a year, $36 for six months, the club currently lists 500 members.

Contact Partners For Travel, P.O. Box 560337, Miami, FL 33256; call 800/866-5565 or 305/661-1878.

Partners In Travel—New President Mary Perez is busy revitalizing this club, the oldest of matchmaker clubs, founded in 1981. Though the club is not limited to mature travelers, about 90% of its members are over 50. The club's newsletter itself is a clearinghouse for correspondents, assigning ID numbers to matchmaker ads and then forwarding mail. Annual dues are $25.

Contact Partners In Travel, 10395A Folsom Blvd. #134, Rancho Cordova, CA 95670; call 800/865-0732.

Travel Companion Exchange (TCE)—Largest club in the country, with almost 3,000 members. TCE President Jens Jensen likes to point out that the larger the club, the more likely you are to find a satisfactory match.

TCE's dues are $99 for eight months, and for that new members get six back issues of the club's newsletter, *Newsletter for Solo Travelers*, so they can start right out with a long listing of current members.

Contact Travel Companion Exchange, P.O. Box 833, Amityville, NY 11701; call 800/392-1256 (from the U.S.) or 516/454-0880 (from Canada).

Another way to find a traveling companion is to advertise. A few travel publications, senior-citizen papers and many local newspapers have travel-companion sections in their classified ads. A few publications key the ads and forward mail—but most don't. That means the people responding to your call for a travel companion are absolutely unscreened: They've filled out no questionnaire, paid no dues, had no interviews—all they have is your phone number or address.

Single-Share Programs

Some cruiselines and tour operators promote

guaranteed-share programs for solo travelers. You are guaranteed the double-occupancy rate—no single-supplement penalty—and the tour organizer tries to match you with a suitable roommate.

At best, you can wind up with no companion at all because the organizer has failed to find you a match. And you'll still pay the lower double-occupancy rate.

At worst, you'll probably wind up with a roommate of the same sex (if that's what you've asked for) who shares your smoking habit (or non-habit) and who wakes up and goes to bed at roughly the same time you do.

Single-share programs are most common on cruiseships. Cruiselines offering them are indicated in the table at the end of this chapter. You don't have to contract the cruiseline—your travel agent can enroll you in the ship's single-share program when you make reservations.

Several tour packagers, especially those organizing trips just for solo travelers, also offer single shares.

Tours Just for Singles

Almost any travel agency can book a singles-only tour for you. But take a good look at the trip brochure before you sign on—for the world of singles-only travel is full of innuendos.

Singleworld Tours are a value, for example, and, we're told, a lot of fun. Though there are no limits on ages of the participants, the Singleworld brochures show lots of robust <u>young</u> adults at play. On the other hand, even if you didn't know that Grand Circle Travel caters only to 49ers+, the photos of enthusiastic seniors in its brochures give you that message. Caveat: Before you sign up for a singles tour, ask your travel agent, "Who goes on these things?" And if the answer doesn't match what the photos in the brochure show, forget it.

Both Grand Circle (800/248-3737) and Saga Holidays (800/343-0273), which also limits its trips to 49ers+, offer single-share plans. Saga also posts a few singles-only departures on its regular tours. On some tours, Saga and Grand Circle may

Solo Travel

waive the single supplements.

Others packaging singles-only trips for mature travelers include:

Mature Tours—This division of a tour packager called Solo Flights organizes escorted tours limited to singles over 50. Mature Tours will try to find you a roommate if you ask, but there is no guaranteed single-share program. Contact Mature Tours, 10 Greenwood Lane, Westport, CT 06430; call 800/266-1566 or 203/256-1235.

Ballroom Dancers Without Partners—This group's trips, mostly cruises, are for men and women over 50 who love to dance. The group provides its own gentlemen hosts when there are not enough single men going along to match the ladies. Often, there is dance instruction for beginners through advanced. There is a single-share plan. Contact Ballroom Dancers Without Partners, 1449 N.W. 15th St., Miami, FL 33125; call 800/778-7953.

Merry Widows—Also packages dance trips for solo women travelers. Trips are slightly more expensive than most, because this group brings along its own gentlemen hosts to make sure ladies always have partners. But there is a single-share plan. Contact Merry Widows Dance Tours, 1515 N. Westshore Blvd., Tampa, FL 33607; call 813/963-2121.

No Supplements At All

The best deal of all for solo travelers are the trips that don't charge any single supplements. There are a few such trips, including most soft adventures on which you camp outdoors—white-water raft trips, horseback journeys, backpack hikes and the like.

Among the cruiselines, World Explorer charges no single supplements on its adventure-learning cruises to places like the Antarctic and Alaska's Inside Passage. Cunard's Prussian Princess also recently posted no supplement for its cruises on European rivers. Posted single supplements for cruiselines are listed in the table at the end of this chapter.

Among tour packagers, Interhostel (800/733-9753) regularly waives single supplements on some of its study trips abroad for 49ers+. Currently Interhostel's 14-day trip to Bristol and London, for example, has no single supplement penalty. Rarely does Interhostel charge a single supplement over 15%.

Elderhostel (617/426-8056), whose learning trips are based mostly on college campuses, are limited to travelers 55+ and cost well under $400 a week, seldom charges single supplements. There is a form of mandatory single-share plan, however. You can request a room by yourself, but you must be willing to share the room with an assigned roommate if none is available.

And before you accept a stranger for a roommate, remember that some mature travelers—even the most gregarious—prefer to pay a little extra for the pleasure of having a private place all their own, to curl up and read a book, to gaze out a porthole or off a balcony, to sneak a nap without fear of interruption.

Sometimes, blessed privacy is worth the cost. ❐

Solo-Friendly Cruiselines

Here are single supplements that cruiselines charge to solo travelers, along with other amenities that appeal to solos. Those that have single-share plans, single cabins and gentleman-host programs:

Cruiseship	Cost	Gent. Host	S'gl. Supp.	S'gl. Cabin	S'gl. Share
American Queen	Mod.	X	75%	X	X
Americana	Mod+		Varies		
Canberra	Mod+		60%		
Caribbean Prince	Low		Varies		
Carnival Destiny	Low		100%	X	X
Celebration	Mod		50%+	X	X
Century	Mod		50%	X	X
Club Med I	Mod		50%		X
Costa Allegra	Mod+		15%+	X	X
Costa Classica	Mod		15%+		X
Costa Romantica	Low		15%+	X	X
Crown Dynasty	Mod+	X	50%	X	X
Costa Victoria	Low		15%	X	X
Crown Odyssey	Mod+	X	60%+	X	X
Crown Princess	Mod		50%	X	X
Cunard Countess	Low		50%	X	X
Cunard Dynasty	Low		50%	X	X
Crystal Harmony	High	X	50%		
Crystal Symph'y	High	X	50%		
Delta Queen	Mod		75%	X	X
Discovery I	Barg		N.A.		
Discovery Sun	Low		N.A.		
Dolphin IV	Barg		50%	X	X
Dreamward	Mod		50%+	X	X
Ecstasy	Low		50%	X	X
Enchanted Isle	Low		50%	X	X
Fair Princess	Mod		50%	X	X
Fantasy	Mod		50%+	X	X
Fascination	Mod		50%	X	X
Golden Princess	Mod		50%	X	X

Cruiseship	Cost	Gent. Host	S'gl. Supp.	S'gl. Cabin	S'gl. Share
Hanseatic	High+		25%		
Holiday	Low		50%+	X	X
Horizon	Mod		50%	X	X
Imagination	Mod		100%	X	X
Independence	Mod	X	60%+	X	X
Inspiration	Mod			X	X
Islandbreeze	Mod		50%		
Island Princess	Mod		50%	X	X
Jubilee	Mod		50%+	X	X
KD River Cruises	Low		50%		
Leg'd of the Seas	Mod	X	50%	X	X
Leeward	Low		10%	X	X
Maasdam	Low	X	25%	X	X
Maj'y of the Seas	Low		50%		X
Marco Polo	Mod	X	25%	X	X
Mayan Prince	Mod		50%		
Mermoz	Low		25%	X	
Meridian	Low		50%	X	X
Miss. Queen	Mod	X	75%	X	X
Monarch of Seas	Mod		50%		X
Nantucket Clipper	Mod		10%+		
Nieuw Am'dam	Low	X	50%	X	X
Noordam	Low	X	50%	X	X
Nordic Empress	Mod		50%		X
Norway	Low		50%	X	X
Norw'n Crown	Mod		50%	X	X
Oceanbreeze	Mod		50%	X	
Oriana	High		60%		
Pacific Princess	Mod		50%	X	X
QE2	Mod	X	15%+	X	
Rad. Diamond	High		25%		
Regal Empress	Barg		50%	X	
Regal Princess	Mod		50%	X	X
Renaissance III	High		30%+	X	
Renaissance IV	High		30%+	X	
Renaissance V	Mod		30%+	X	
Rotterdam	Low	X	35%	X	X
Royal Majesty	Mod		50%		
Royal Odyssey	Mod		60%+	X	X
Royal Princess	Mod		50%	X	X
Royal Seas	Mod		100%		
Royal Vik. Queen	Mod		100%	X	
Royal Vik. Sun	High	X	25%+	X	X

Solo Travel

Cruiseship	Cost	Gent. Host	S'gl. Supp.	S'gl. Cabin	S'gl. Share
Ryndam	Low	X	50%	X	X
Sc'vian Dawn	Mod		100%		
Sea Bird	Mod		25%		
Sea Goddess I	Mod		15%	X	X
Sea Goddess II	High		15%		X
Sea Lion	High		25%		
Seabourn L'g'nd	High		10%		
Seabourn Pride	High		10%		
Seabourn Spirit	HIgh+		10%		
Seabreeze I	High		50%	X	
Seaward	Mod		50%	X	X
Sensation	Mod		50%+	X	X
Silver Cloud	High	X	10%+		
Silver Wind	High	X	10%		
Sky Princess	Mod		50%	X	X
Song of America	Low		50%		X
Song of Flower	High		25%+		
Song of Norway	Mod		50%		X
Sov. of Seas	Mod		50%		X
Spirit of Alaska	Mod		50%		
Spirit of C'l'mbia	Mod		50%		
Spirit of Disc.	Low		50%		
Spirit of Gl. Bay	Mod		50%		
Spirit of '98	Mod		50%		
Star Clipper	Mod		50%		
Star Flyer	Mod		50%		
Star Odyssey	Mod	X	60%+	X	X
Star Princess	Low		50%	X	X
Starship Atlantic	Low		75%	X	
Starship Oceanic	Low		75%	X	
Statendam	Low	X	50%	X	X
Stella Solaris	Low		50%+		X
Sun Princess	Mod.		100%	X	X
Sun Viking	Mod		50%		X
Sun Viking	Mod		50%		X
Triton	Mod		50%	X	X
Tropicale	Low		50%+	X	X
Tropicana	Low		N.A.		
Universe Expl.	Low		None	X	
Veendam	Low	X	50%	X	X
Viking Princess	Mod		50%		
Viking Serenade	Low		50%		X
Vistafjord	Mod	X	15%+	X	

Cruiseship	Cost	Gent. Host	S'gl. Supp.	S'gl. Cabin	S'gl. Share
Westerdam	Low	X	35%	X	X
Wilderness Expl.	Barg		50%		
Wind Song	High		50%		
Wind Spirit	High		50%		
Wind Star	High		50%		
Windward	Mod		50%	X	X
World Ren.	Mod		50%	X	X
Yorktown Clipper	Mod		50%		
Zenith	Low		50%	X	X

9. Low-Cost and No-Cost Ways to Go

If you're addicted to traveling, at least you can sign up for some of these special budget-saving trips.

For many, travel is habit-forming. Some mature travelers just can't get enough. Yet, there are not many who can afford to take a $5,000 trip each month.

Even so, mature travelers can stay on the road for many, many days without busting their budgets.

Elderhosteling

Elderhostel learning trips are so addictive that many mature travelers attend four or five sessions a year in different parts of the country, or sign up for two sessions back-to-back. It's not just the cost that's appealing—you get a week's room and board in a college or resort setting, usually for little more than $50 a day.

Travelers who can't afford even the low cost of Elderhosteling can apply for low-cost "Hostelship" scholarships.

A quarter-million-or-more seniors participate in Elderhostel sessions each year at more than 1,800 locations in the United States and Canada. Elderhostel is limited to participants 55+ and their spouses over 50.

A typical Elderhostel format is this one by Mohave Community College at Lake Havasu, Ariz.: Students gather on Sunday and, starting Monday, spend five days taking courses from college faculty members in History of Medieval Art forms (the meeting site is next door to the Medieval London Bridge), Astronomy and Basic Videography. Each course meets for 1-1/2 hours a day. There are also short enrichment sessions on other topics.

Students live on campus, usually in dormitory rooms (one or two to a room) and take most meals at student commons. The Lake Havasu session costs $385 a person—including lodging and meals, touring and instruction.

At other Elderhostels, students can learn anything from downhill skiing and big-band jazz to paleontology and the architecture of Frank Lloyd Wright. While most Elderhostels are on college campuses, some are at remote conference centers, ski resorts and even on the trail (there are even white-water rafting and canoeing Elderhostels).

Special-format elderhostels—grandparent/grandchild sessions, programs for hearing-impaired, RV Elderhostels (which are less expensive, because you stay in your own "housing") and a few intensive, one-topic sessions—are also offered.

Elderhostel publishes four free, seasonal *United States and Canada Catalogs* each year. To get on the mailing list, contact Elderhostel, 75 Federal St., Boston, Ma 02110; call 617/426-5437.

There are also international Elderhostel programs and Elderhostel Service Programs for travelers 55+. While these are enriching study programs, they do not represent the great bargains for mature travelers that domestic Elderhostels do.

Group Tour Leaders

When Dean and Jackie Evans of West Chester, Pa., went to northern Italy with 29 friends—Rome, Sorrento, Florence, Venice, Milan, plus a side-trip into Switzerland—they paid a perfect price:

Nothing. Zip. Zero.

The trip, including airfare, was free.

George and Kay Herzog of the Sun City West retirement community near Phoenix, Ariz., took a five-day cruise to Mexico for that same price.

The Evanses and the Herzogs were tour group leaders. Tour group leaders gather groups of travelers who pay full fare, and for each 10 to 14 clients who accompany them, one person goes free. Any mature traveler with good organizational

No-Cost Travel

skills, who likes people, can handle details and isn't afraid to speak up when necessary, can do the same thing.

You can recruit travelers from your church, retirement community, Rotary club, bridge club—or just friends and neighbors—to create tour groups. Some inveterate group leaders even use newspaper ads or send out press releases.

Almost all tour companies provide free or discounted passage for group leaders. But their policies vary widely. Here are two examples:

Grand Circle Travel, specializing in trips for 49ers+, offers one free placc on an escorted tour or an extended-vacation trip for any group leader who enrolls 10 other travelers at full price, or 15 travelers at group-discounted prices. For cruises, GCT offers one free cabin for every 15 sold at full price, or 20 at discounted prices. Contact GCT, 347 Congress St., Boston, MA 02210; call 800/248-3737.

EF Educational Tours specializes in educational tours, mostly to Europe, for teachers and students, but the company also will tailor group tours to other areas. Fully paid groups of six earn the group leader a seventh passage. The leader's family members earn a 15% discount. EF's *Counselor Recruitment Handbook* is a good resource for potential group leaders. Contact EF Educational Tours, One Memorial Dr., Cambridge, MA 02142; call 800/637-8222.

You can also organize a group trip through your own travel agent.

Great resources for group travel leaders planning shorter domestic trips are organizations like Southern California's Senior Travel Recreation and Activities Council, called "STRAC" (619/341-6722), or Group Leaders of America (606/253-0455) in the Midwest. These groups stage marketplaces and put out newsletters in which travel vendors advertise their group discounts and deals for leaders and their bus drivers.

There is also help from some major tour packagers, like Nevada's Frontier Travel & Tours (702/882-2100), which have clubs that meet regularly and newsletters that promote trips to group leaders.

But veteran group leaders give this advice: Pick the destination first, then contact several tour companies that go there--instead of the other way around.

Outdoor Volunteers

Many mature travelers stay free for weeks—and even months—in some of North America's prettiest places. They join a growing number of outdoor volunteers who help other visitors to the nation's state and national parks and forests.

While most of these thousands of volunteers become campground hosts, help is also needed to put on costumes and fire Brown Bess muskets (at Moores Creek National Battlefield in North Carolina), to keep a lighthouse (on Wisconsin's Apostle Islands), to clean headstones (at Maryland's Antietam National Battlefield), to help golfers (at four Georgia state parks), to maintain trails, to answer questions at visitor centers and to drive buses.

The number of outdoor volunteer jobs is increasing rapidly. Many programs, like those at Georgia and Virginia state parks, are new. One reason, a U.S. Forest Service spokesman says, is budget cutbacks at federal and state levels.

And you don't have to be an RVer to be a volunteer.

Campground hosting jobs are simple: welcome visitors, show them to campsites and answer questions about the area. For that, volunteers get free RV campsites including hookups, where available, free use of park facilities and time off to explore on their own. At Alaska's Mendenhall Glacier, volunteers get allowances up to $23 a day and round-trip transportation from Seattle. Under Georgia's "Golf Course Ranger" program, volunteers get free rounds of golf on public courses.

No-Cost Travel

Most volunteer jobs require a commitment of two or three months, though some can last as little as two weeks.

Volunteers are needed year-round, not just in summers. Helpers who know how to snowmobile are needed to groom ski trails in Alaska's Chugash National Forest. At Vicksburg National Military Park, RVers get free campsites, with hookups, all year in return for helping to clean trails. State and national campgrounds throughout the South seek volunteer winter hosts.

Those who don't travel in RVs are not shut out of volunteer jobs. Places like Alaska's Tongass National Forest, California's Death Valley National Monument and Michigan's Isle Royale National Park offer volunteers free lodging in cabins or bunkhouses.

Most outdoor volunteer jobs are available through district offices of the U.S. Park Service, the U.S. Forest Service and the Bureau of Land Management, state park services and private agencies like the Sierra Club, Student Conservation Association and Appalachian Mountain Club.

Many RVers hear about volunteer jobs from fellow campers, or simply stop at a park or forest service district office in an area they like and ask what's available. But more systematic volunteers buy an annual copy of The American Hiking Society's directory, *Helping Out in the Outdoors*, and search it for new places to go.

The *Helping Out* directory lists hundreds of places where volunteers are needed, a description of the area, the kind of work to be done, time required, a description of the campsite or housing provisions and other compensation, along with contact information. To find an outdoor volunteer job, AHS recommends these steps:

• Decide where you want to be: what state or region, what kind of work, and for how long?

• From the *Helping Out* directory, pick the two or three jobs that you like best. Write or call the contact person listed to make sure volunteers are still needed.

- In your letter or call, get all your questions answered: What kind of weather should you be ready for? What equipment do you bring? Is there reimbursement for out-of-pocket expenses? Is there a food allowance? How long will the assignment last?
- When you are accepted, show up on the appointed day as agreed. The agency is counting on you to be there.

For a copy of the *Helping Out* directory, which is updated every November, send $7 to the American Hiking Society, P.O. Box 20160, Washington, DC 20041-2160.

Other Traveling Jobs

There are ways to take trips and actually get paid for it—after all, people like highway patrol troopers, traveling salesmen and truck drivers do it all the time. But that's not really traveling; that's working.

There are, however, some jobs that hardly seem like real work, that allow mature travelers to see new places and actually come home with a few pennies more than they left with.

At Sun City West near Phoenix we met Sammy and Lorena Dimarco, who had spent the summer working in the gift shop at Old Faithful Lodge in Yellowstone Park. "They recruit summer help at colleges," explained Lorena Dimarco, "but they'll take anyone who has a summer to give. We visited there the year before, and decided we wanted to come back. So we just went down to the personnel office and asked . . . "

During their summer in Yellowstone, the Dimarcos had enough time to tour the park, visit nearby Jackson Hole and do a lot of fishing (her hobby) and birdwatching (his hobby). The Dimarcos, of course, got paid for their work.

We met Billy McGrady, a retired electrician from Cleveland, at a KOA Kampground near Mobile, Ala. McGrady is a full-time RVer, but often he comes to rest at a campground that can use his services. He had been at the Mobile-area campground about six weeks, rewiring some campsites, helping out in the store—and fishing the bayous, his passion. Soon, he said, he'd be leaving for Atlanta, where he'd lined up another few weeks of work at a campground. "Down here in winter, up north in summer is my motto," said McGrady.

Fish and get paid for it? Ski and get paid for it? Why not?

Dimarcos were playing on the obvious fact that seasonal crowds of travelers generate need for seasonal help: summer workers at resorts like Old Faithful and winter workers at ski areas like Vail and Squaw Valley. While their method was haphazard—just go and apply—their instincts were good.

McGrady's travel-job hunt is more systematic, and typical of those who want to earn extra bucks while they travel. They read *Workcamper News*, an every-other-month newsletter that lists job opportunities that actually pay money—including many temporary ones like McGrady's and the Dimarcos'—at campgrounds, resorts, within parks and forests and wherever campers go. Though it's especially popular among full-time RVers, you don't have to be an RVer to subscribe.

For a sample copy write *Workcamper News*, 201 Hiram Road, Heber Springs, AR 726543; call 501/362-2637. Send $23 for a year's subscription.

Other Ways to Work for Your Supper

If you call ballroom dancing, demonstrating your golf game or teaching your favorite hobby "work," then here is another way to "work" for your next trip.

Every cruiseline—and a few resorts—look for people with special skills. If you can teach hula dancing, basket-weaving, languages, bridge, tennis or whatever, there's a chance for a mature traveler to get a free (or almost free) vacation.

To find these "jobs," contact the cruiselines' headquarters offices, tell them what you can do and ask how you can sign on. As an alternative, one agency recruits people with special skills. In addition to conducting gentleman-host programs for many major cruiselines (see Chapter 4), Lauretta Blake's The Working Vacation agency also recruits others with special skills to lecture and teach at sea.

Contact the agency at 610 Pine Grove Court, New Lenox, IL 60451; call 815/485-8307.

You may have to pay a sign-up fee, plus a current charge of $150 a week for the time you're on the "job"—that is, the length of your cruise.

Just don't say travel isn't work. ❐

10. Bargains Galore In Mature Travelers' Favorite Places

Savvy travelers tend to return to destinations that are senior-friendly and provide the best value.

There are places mature travelers return to time and time again: Hawaii, the Caribbean, Alaska, San Francisco and London lead the list. That's probably because savvy travelers have seen a lot of the world, and tend to return to favorite places—places they have learned are senior-friendly and provide the best value.

Each year *The Mature Traveler* newsletter surveys its readers to compile a list of mature travelers' favorite trips and destinations. It is not a scientific sampling, but does reveal strong preferences

Any reader of this book can vote for a favorite destination or trip by using the coupon at the end of this chapter and mailing it to *The Mature Traveler*, P.O. Box 50400, Reno, NV 89513-0400. If you are not a subscriber but want to see how your favorites compared with others', send $5 for the January issue of *TMT*, where results of the survey are printed.

The list of favorite destinations has not changed much since 1988, when *TMT* began making its annual survey: Spain was dropped a few years ago, probably because of the soaring cost of travel there. England and Ireland moved to the top of the list when "The Troubles" officially ended.

San Francisco and London typically see-saw as mature travelers' favorite cities.

A few great trips favored by mature travelers are relatively expensive: Steamboatin' on America's vast inland river system, the Orient Express through Europe or the excursion train from Tucson to Mexico's Copper Canyon come to mind. Cut-rate fares on these trips are rare, and they offer no senior discounts. But these are once-in-a-lifetime trips, and worth saving for.

For the most part, though, mature travelers' favorite places are inexpensive and provide great value in experience and price. Most offer a wide array of age-based discounts that can cut costs 20%-to-30%—sometimes up to half. Here are some of the best deals available to mature travelers' in mature travelers' favorite places:

1. Great Britain—Frames Rickards London Tour company gives travelers 55+ 5% discounts on Great Britain, Ireland tour packages. See your travel agent . . . Tourist Trail Pass lets 49ers+ ride National Express and Scottish Citylink cross-country buses for 20-25% off. Get Tourist Trail Passes from your travel agent or British Tourist Office before you leave the U.S. 800/462-2748 . . . Travelers 60+ get 15-20% discounts on BritRail Senior Flexpasses and BritRail Senior Classic Passes, good for trains anywhere in the U.K. Get passes from your travel agent before you go or from BritRail, 800/677-8585. BritRail Senior Railcard, costing £16, gives holders 60+ one-third off railfares; you must buy the Senior Railcard in the U.K.

Ireland: Travelers 55+ get $55 off CIE escorted tours. 800/243-8687 . . . Visitors 60+ get £3 off £10 Heritage Card, giving admission to 10 favorite attractions in Dublin. 212/418-0800 . . . Seniors get 50 pence off £1.50 admission to Jerpoint Abbey, £2 admission to the Waterford Crystal Showroom, £2 admission to Lismore Heritage Centre, Waterford and £2.50 Kilkenny City walking tours . . . Visitors 60+ to Cobh Heritage Centre get £1 off £3.50 admission.

2. Hawaii—Passengers 55+ get 15% off Royal Hawaiian Cruises' day-trips through the islands that

Senior-Friendly Places

range from $45 to $135. 800/852-4183 . . . Outrigger Hotels throughout the islands, including 20 on Waikiki and the Royal Waikoloan on the Big Island, give 20% discounts to travelers 50+, another 5% off to AARP members. Call toll-free 800/733-7777 . . . Hilton Hawaiian Village and other Hiltons on the Islands take part in the chain's Senior HHonors program, giving guests 60+ room discounts of 25%-to-50%, plus other perks . . . Hawaii's Sheraton Hotels, including the Waikiki Sheraton and freshly restored Royal Hawaiian, honor the company's Golden Guest 25% discount program for travelers 60+. 800/325-3535.

"Sun Club" deal gives travelers 55+ 25% or more off rooms at all Aston Hotels and Resorts in Hawaii. 800/922-7866 . . . Hawaiiana Resorts, with hotels on Waikiki and condos on Maui, give AARP members and others 60+ 10%-to-25% discounts. A condo on Maui, for example, can cost seniors as little as $75 a night. Call 800/367-7040 . . . Hyatt Regency Resorts on Oahu, Maui and Kauai honor the company's 25% discount program for travelers 62+. 800/233-1234 . . . 19 Castle Resorts and Hawaiian Pacific Resorts give 49ers+ deep discounts, depending on season, at hotels and condos on major islands. Example: a room at Maui Palms hotel for as little as $41. A rental car with unlimited mileage is $10 a day extra. 800/367-5004.

Kauai: Guests 55+ get 10% off $100-$175 rooms at Hanalei Colony Resort. Seventh night is free. 808-826-6235 . . . Coconut Beach Resort gives travelers 55+ 30% off $125-$175 rooms. 800/222-5642.

Maui: AARP members get 30% off regular $195-to-$295 room rates at Royal Lahaina Resort on Kaanapali Beach. Other guests 55+ get 20% off. 800/447-6925 . . . Hana Plantation Houses gives AARP members 10% off $70-$160 rooms. 800/228-4262 . . . Three Village Resorts condos at Kaanapali and West Maui give AARP members and other guests 60+ 10% discounts. 800/367-7052.

Oahu: Waikiki Parkside gives 49ers+ 30%-to-40% off rooms that regularly cost $104 to $130. 800/237-9666 . . . Guests 60+ get 25% of $140-$180 rooms, plus 10% off meals, at Alana Waikiki Hotel; no blackout dates. 800/367-6070 . . . Guests 55+ and AARP members get 20% off $170 rooms at Hawaiian Regent Hotel on Waikiki. 800/367-5370 . . . Ala Moana Hotel, on the edge of Waikiki, gives guests 55+ 25% off $120-$145 rooms, plus discounts at hotel restaurants. 800/367-6025 . . . Royal Garden hotel on Waikiki gives travelers 60+ $120 rooms for $85. 800/367-5666 . . . The Colony Surf Hotel at the far end of Waikiki gives AARP members 25% discounts off rooms that range from $125-to-$315. 808/923-5751 . . . 49ers+ get 25% off rooms that regularly cost $185-$280 a night at Ilikai Hotel, overlooking Honolulu's Yacht Harbor. Ilikai also offers a "Senior Value Package," including dinner for two and one-bedroom suite, for $138.75 a night. Call 800/367-8434.

3. New Zealand—Travelers 60+ get half or more off—savings of $2,000 or more—on autumn's late-season ski tours, early golf tours from Tour New Zealand. 800/822-5494 . . . 49ers+ get $3 off day-long $8.50 City Sights Trambus tour of Brisbane, with pickups around downtown . . . Most other senior discounts, which are numerous, are limited to New Zealand residents.

4. Alaska—Passengers 65+ get half-off fares between all Alaska ports on Alaska Marine Highway ferries Oct. 1-April 30. Passage for seniors is $5 between some ports all year. Call 800/642-0066 . . . Travelers 65+ get 25% off fares on Alaska Railroad mid-September to mid-May. 800/544-0552 for reservations . . . Travelers 65+ get $100 off cost of AlaskaPass from Oct. 1-April 30. 800/248-7598 . . . AARP members get $50 off $2,295-$2,895 cost of Alaska Senior Safaris. 800/334-8730 . . . Golfers 60+ get $14 off $38 green fees at Alyeska Resort near Girdwood. 907/754-2216.

5. Caribbean—Passengers 65+ and cabin-mates of

Senior-Friendly Places

any age get 10%-to-15% off fares on Premier Cruise Lines Bahamas cruises from east Florida ports. In fall discounts for mature travelers often are deeper. 800/327-7113 . . . Costa Cruises gives passengers 60+ 10% discounts on tickets purchased at least 90 days before the cruise. 800/327-2537 . . . Passengers 55+ get 10% discounts on week-long voyages of the tall ship Sir Francis Drake that regularly cost $895-$995. Deal is good through June 1997. 800/662-0090.

Bahamas: Passengers 65+ get $14 off $74 fare for Atlantis Submarines tour out of Nassau. 800/253-0493.

Puerto Rico: Hotel Condado Beach and sister hotel, La Concho, in San Juan offer 25% discounts on $160 rooms year-round for travelers 60+. 800/468-2775.

Turks & Caicos: Guests 55+ get 10% off $150-$405 rooms at Ocean Club Resort in low seasons, May-June and September-November. 800/457-8787.

6. Florida—Fort Lauderdale: Visitors 65+ get $1 off $8.50 combination (all-inclusive) ticket at Museum of Discovery and Science and Imax Theater. 209/658-8687.

Orlando Area: Travelers 55+ get 10% off $39.95 admission at Sea World of Florida. 407/363-2613 . . . Visitors 55+ to Orlando's Wet 'n Wild amusement park get half off regular $23.95 admission; grandkids get $3 off. Call 407/351-3200 . . . 49ers+ get 10% off $33.95 meal-and-admission to Sleuths Mystery Dinner Show. Call 407/363-1985 . . . Flower lovers 55+ get $1 off $8.95 admission to A World of Orchids garden at Kissimmee. 407/396-1881.

✓ AARP members and other guests 65+ at Peabody Orlando pay $89—more than half off—for rooms that regularly cost $230. 800/732-2639.

Universal Studios at Orlando gives 15% off its $38.50 general admission price to visitors 55+ who enroll in "Silver Stars Club," plus up to five guests. Members also get 10% off merchandise, 15% off meals. The club is free. 407/363-8217 . . . AARP members get 10% discounts off villa rentals around Kissimmee from Feel Like Home. 800/726-0434 . . . Two Holiday Inns near Disney World offer age-based "Senior Fun Club" discounts: $10 off for every decade of age over 50. Deals are at Sun Spree Resort (800/800/366-6299) and Main Gate East (800/366-5437).

St. Augustine: Marineland of Florida gives visitors 55+ 20% off $14.95 admission price. 904/471-1111 . . . Seniors get $1 off $4.50 admission to the Fountain of Youth Archaeological Park, where Ponce de Leon came ashore in 1513 . . . Visitors 55+ also get $1 off $5 admission to Zorayda Castle. 904/824-3097 . . . Mature travelers get 50¢ off $5 admission to North America's oldest house (904/824-2872) and its oldest wooden school house (904/824-0192) . . . Seniors get 75¢ off $5.50 admission to Potter's Wax Museum (904/829-9056).

Tampa: Seniors get free admission to Bay Downs racetrack on Thursdays. 813/855-4401 . . . Visitors 55+ get 15% off $36.15 admission to Busch Gardens . . . 49ers+ also get 15% off $20.95 admission to Adventure Island. 813/987-5660.

Winter Haven: Visitors 55+ get 15% off $29.63 day-long admission admission to Cypress Gardens. 800/282-2123.

Mature Travelers' Favorite Cities

Here are some of the best discounts for mature travelers in their favorite cities:

1. San Francisco Bay Area—Blue & Gold Fleet (415/705-5444) gives travelers 62+ $8 off $16 fare for bay cruises. Red & White Fleet (415/546-2628) gives visitors 62+ $1.75 off $10 Alcatraz cruise, $4 off $16 Golden Gate cruise . . . Visitors 60+ get $1.50 off $8.50 admission to Ripley's Believe It or Not Museum. 415/771-6188 . . . The Muni sells travelers 65+ $8 monthly Fastpasses to ride cable cars, buses and streetcars. Regular cable-car fare is $2. Buy passes at the Muni office, Geary and Presidio streets . . . Visitors 65+ get $16 worth of rides on the BART (the subway) for $4. Buy passes at Safeway or Lucky grocery stores, or by mail from BART, 800 Madison St., Oakland, CA 94607 . . . Gray Line Sightseeing

Senior-Friendly Places

Tours gives S.F. visitors 60+ $2 off any tour, 15% off for AARP members. 415/558-9400

✓ **Hotel Union Square gives guests 62+ $102 rooms for $69. Call 800/553-1900.**

Modest Hotel Bedford, also near Union Square, gives 49ers+ $109 rooms for $84-$90, plus other frequent deals, like 3-nights-for-the-price of 2. 800/227-5642 . . . 49ers+ get $139-$249 rooms for $105 at Cartwright Hotel, a boutique hotel near Union Square. 800/227-3844. Deal includes two California State Lottery tickets . . . Carlton Hotel, near Union Square, gives AARP members and other guests 62+ $125 rooms for $109 a night, and fifth night is free—a total cost of $436 for five nights. 800/227-4496 . . . AARP members and others 60+ pay $105 a night for $125 rooms at Villa Florence hotel on Union Square. 800/553-4411. . . Tuscan Inn, luxury motel at Fisherman's Wharf, gives 49ers+ $158 rooms for $113. 800/648-4626.

San Jose: 49ers+ get $2 off $6 admission to the Rosicrucian Egyptian Museum; $3 off $12.50 admission to the Winchester Mystery House; $9 off $27.95 admission to Paramount's Great Adventure theme park; and 20% off lower-priced seating at the San Jose Symphony. 800/726-5673.

San Mateo: AARP members at Dunphy Hotel get $140 rooms for as little as $65. 415/573-7661.

2. London—At Cabinet War Rooms and Imperial War Museum 49ers+ get 25% off $6 admission price. 800/462-2748 . . . Military retirees from any NATO country get nice rooms at Waterloo district's Union Jack Club (call 011 44 0171 928-6401 for reservations) and Victory Services Club (011 44 0171 723-4474) near Marble Arch for as little as $30 a night . . . Seniors get £1 off £4 guided walks from London Walks, 0171-794-1764 . . . Visitors 60+ get one-third off £8.50 admission price at Buckingham Palace—whenever it's open.

3. Paris—*Carte Vermeil* costing $28 for four trips, $52 for unlimited trips, gives travelers 60+ half-off rail fares for a year, including TGV service, during off-peak times, 20% at peak times. *Carte* also is good for free or cut-rate admission to museums (including the Louvre), other attractions. Buy the card at the railroad station.

4. Las Vegas Area—Visitors 62+ ride CAT (Citizens Area Transit) buses throughout the city for half off $1 fare . . . Visitors 60+ get $2 off $7 elevator ride to the new Stratosphere Tower, more than 1,000 feet up. If you have lunch or dinner reservations, the elevator ride is free. 800/998-6937 . . . Visitors 60+ get $6 off $15 ride-and-entertainment passes at Wizard of Oz theme park at MGM Grand Hotel. 702/891-1111 . . . Grey Line gives 49ers+ $2.50 off tours of the city, Hoover Dam and Lake Mead Cruises costing $17.95-$31.60, $6 off $95 Hoover Dam land/air tour. 702/384-1234 . . . Visitors 55+ to Wet 'n Wild theme park on the Strip get half of $21.95 admission. 702/871-7811 . . . Visitors 55+ get $2 off $6 admission at Ceasars Palace Omnimax. 702/731-7110 . . . 49ers+ pay $3 admission to Imperial Palace Auto Collection, regularly $6.75. 800/634-6441 . . . Liberace Museum gives visitors 60+ $2 off $6.50 admission. 702/789-5595 . . . 49ers+ get 50¢ off $1.50 admission to Clark County Heritage Museum in Henderson. 702/455-7955 . . . 49ers+ get $1 off $4.95 admission to Guinness World of Records Museum (702/792-3766), $1 off $5 admission at Las Vegas Natural History Museum (702/384-3466) and 10% off $5 admission to Lied Discovery Children's Museum (702/382-5437).

✓ Fitzgerald's Casino/Hotel downtown offers room discounts to guests 55+ which vary by season. Example: $64-$190 rooms as low as $20-$34 (double) in the fall, $30 in January. 800/274-5825 for current deals. Hotel has 33 rooms for handicapped.

St. Tropez Resort gives AARP members 25%-to-30% off regular rates. 800/666-5400 . . . Members of Four Queens' free "Club 55 Slot Club" get 15% off $54-$65 room rates, 10% off at restaurants, bars and gift shops, room rates. Visit the hospitality desk to join.

Senior-Friendly Places

702/385-4011 . . . "Sunrise Senior Club" members get $59-$79 rooms for $39 at Melrose Suites hotel, near the Strip, and $49 rooms for $32 at Sunrise Suites hotel on the Boulder Highway. 800/362-4040 to join the club; membership is free . . . Nevada Palace on the Boulder Highway gives members of its free "Silver Circle" slots club $5 off $35-$50 rooms, 10% discounts at restaurants. Just go in to join. 800/634-6283. Guests 55+ get $91 rooms for $63 at Bally's Las Vegas on center-Strip. 800/634-3434 . . . Seven-night Vacation Villa stays at Del Webb's Sun City Summerlin cost guests 55+ $491, including a round of golf and use of rec facilities. 800/987-9875 . . . Attractive room discounts in Las Vegas under their chains' corporate programs at Flamingo Hilton, Desert Inn (Sheraton), Marriott's Residence Inn, Quality Inn, Travelodge, Days Inn are listed in Chapter 2.

Mesquite: Guests 60+ get 10% off $39 weeknight room rates at Oasis Resort Hotel-Casino. 800/621-0187 . . . Members of Players Island Resort/Casino's "50 Plus" club get 20% off $42 rooms, plus discounts on meals, the spa and golf rates. 800/882-6216.

5. New York City—Visitors 65+ ride MTA buses and subways for half-price. You may have to show Medicare card. 212/878-3000 . . . Visitors 65+ get $2 off $7 admission to The Jewish Museum. 212/423-3200 . . . Ferry ride and admission to the Statue of Liberty/Ellis Island Immigration Museum, regularly $7, is $5 for 49ers+. 212/363-3209 . . . 49ers+ get $1 off $6 admission to South Street Seaport Museum. 212/669-9400 . . . Seniors get $2 off $4 admission to Empire State Building observation deck. 212/736-3100 . . . 49ers+ get $2 off $6.50 tour of the United Nations Headquarters. 212/963-7713.

Seniors+ get $2 off $5 admission to Pierpont Morgan Library 212/685-0008 . . . Guests 65+ get $6.75 admission to Bronx Zoo for $3. 718/367-1010 . . . Seniors get $3 off $8 admission to Museum of Modern Art. 212/708-9480 . . . Visitors 65+ get $3 off $7 admission to Solomon R. Guggenheim Museum. 212/360-3500 . . . Also $3.50 off $7 Metropolitan Museum of Art admission. 212/535-7710 . . . $6 trip to World Trade Center Observation Deck costs visitors 65+ $3.50. 212/435-7397 . . . 50¢ round-trip on Staten Island Ferry costs 49ers+ 25¢

... Seniors get $2 off $8 admission to Whitney Museum of American Art. (212/570-3676), $2 off $7 admission to Hayden Planetarium (212/769-5922), $1 off $6 admission for Carnegie Hall tours (212/903-9600).

6. Seattle Area—Visitors 65+ pay $3 for lifetime pass on Metro Buses entitling them to fare of a 25¢ ride. Get pass at Westlake Center, Third & Pine, or Metro Transit Office, 821 Second Ave. 206/553-3060 ... Passengers 62+ get 15% off $42 round-trip fare on the Mt. Baker International, new, high-tech excursion train between Seattle and Vancouver, B.C. 800/872-7245 ... Travelers 65+ get $10 off $89 round-trip fare on Victoria Clipper between Seattle and Victoria, B.C. 800/888-2535 ... Travelers 65+ get $3-$10 discounts on Puget Sound cruises and bicycle-cruises aboard Mosquito Fleet boats. 800/325-6722 ... Visitors 65+ get half off $4 tour of Kingdome stadium near downtown. 206/296-3128 ... Visitors 60+ get $1 off $6.50 Underground Tours. 206/682-4646 ... Space Needle visitors 65+ get $2 off the $8.50 elevator ride to the top. 800/937-9582 ... Visitors 62+ save $3 on $45 cruise-tours to Tillicum Village, which include a salmon bake and Indian dancing; 360/377-8924 ... The Seattle Aquarium gives visitors 65+ $1.45 off $7.15 admission; 206/386-4320 ... Visitors 65+ save $1.75 on $7.50 regular admission to Woodland Park Zoo; 206/684-4800 ... 49ers+ get $2 off $6 admission to Seattle Art Museum. 206/654-3100.

Guests 55+ at Alexis Hotel get 15%-to-20% off rooms regularly costing $155-$300 a night. Deal includes passes to Seattle Art Museum. 800/426-7033 ... Hotel Vintage Park offers 49ers+ $175 rooms for $125. 800/624-4433 ... Guests 55+ get 10% discounts on $80-$80 rooms at Pacific Plaza Hotel. 800/426-1165 ... Guests 55+ at Seattle's Warwick Hotel get one-third off regular $190 room rates. 800/426-9280.

<u>Bremerton</u>: Kitsap Harbor Tours gives visitors 62+ $2 off $11.50 shipyard-tour cruises, $1 off $5 admission to destroyer Turner Joy, moored nearby. 360/377-8924.

<u>Tacoma</u>: Kimpton's Sheraton Tacoma hotel gives seniors 22% off $143 rooms. 800/325-35354.❐

Vote For Your Favorite Places

The Mature Traveler conducts a running survey of favorite places of 49ers+. Please vote for your own favorites below:

- **What Are Your Three Favorite Destinations?**
  - ____ England & the U.K.
  - ____ Hawaii
  - ____ New Zealand or Australia
  - ____ Alaska
  - ____ The Caribbean Area
  - ____ Florida
  - ____ Mexico
  - ____ Canada. Where?_____
  - ____ Elsewhere in the U.S._____
  - ____ Elsewhere in Europe:_____
  - ____ Elsewhere in Asia: _____
  - ____ Elsewhere in the world: _____

- What makes a place your favorite? ___ Low cost? ___ Sightseeing? ___ Shopping? ___ Climate? ___ Activities (like golf or swimming)? Other: _____

- Or would you rather be (please pick one): ___ Cruising? ___ Steamboatin'? ___ Motorcoaching? ___ Riding a train? ___ Driving? ___RVing?

- What is your favorite city anywhere?

_____

- What is the best travel discount for mature travelers you've found in the last 18 months? _____

- How often do you travel?
___ More than 4 times a year? ___ 2-3 times a year? ___ Once a year? ___ Less than once?

Send your completed ballot to: *The Mature Traveler*, P.O. Box 50400, Reno, NV 89513-0400.
Fax 702/786-7856, or e-mail MatureTrav@aol.com.

The Book of Deals is Free When You Subscribe to *TMT*

Great discounts for mature travelers come and go in the blink of an eye. Now that you know how senior discounts work and what's available, if you are serious travelers you need to be alert to new deals that are offered all the time.

You need *The Mature Traveler* monthly newsletter—the only way to keep up-to-date on current discounts just for 49ers+, great trips for mature travelers and senior-friendly places.

Every month it's chock-full of <u>new</u> discounts for mature travelers, just like the ones you've read about in this book.

And we're going to make you an offer you can't refuse:

We're going to give you back <u>all</u> the money you spent on this copy of *The Mature Traveler's Book of Deals* when you subscribe to our newsletter, *The Mature Traveler*!

Send in the coupon below with your check or credit-card authorization, and you get back the full retail price of this book—$7.95 off *TMT's* annual subscription price of $29.95.

WHAT A DEAL!

☐ **YES! Please enter my one-year subscription (12 issues) to *The Mature Traveler* for just $22—$7.95 off the yearly subscription price of $29.95.**

☐ **Charge my ____ Visa Card ____ Mastercard**

Card No._____ Expires_____

My Signature_____
(Required for charge-card purchase)

☐ **My Payment is Enclosed**

My Name _____

Address _____

City, State, ZIP_____

Telephone No. _____

**Mail Today to: The Mature Traveler,
P.O. Box 50400, Reno, NV 89513-0400**

11. Nickels and Dimes: Deals That Are Just Plain Fun

These discounts don't influence travel plans, but it's nice to know about them when you're in the neighborhood.

As readers have seen, mature travelers get discounts wherever they go. They can save a thousand dollars a couple barging through Europe, hundreds of dollars by picking the right tour, hundreds more by traveling at the right time, choosing the right cruiseship or joining the right club. These are the kind of deals that can make travel plans, deals that save big money.

But for every discount big enough to influence plans, there must be 10 or more that don't.

They're what we call "Nickels and Dimes." They're discounts for mature travelers that are just fun to find, things like half-price golf in Alaska, $5 off a whale-watching tour you'd probably take even if there weren't a discount, 60% off at the La Brea Tar Pits, a $10.50 saving on a chocolate factory tour; free admission to museums in Dublin, a buck off San Francisco's Alcatraz tour or The Sixth Floor Kennedy assassination museum in Dallas. Fun places, with honest though modest discounts.

We traveled to San Francisco with friends who had just turned 50. They made fun of us all the way while we each saved $2.85 on the cable car, $3 on a submarine tour, $3 on a bay cruise and $1.20 at a museum simply by showing our AARP card. That's a little over $10, and it more than paid for a good lunch. The capper, of course, came the next morning when we settled our hotel bill: Our friends' came to $35 more than ours, though we had the same kind of rooms.

Simply because, when we made reservations-- where else we went-- we asked for the senior discount. And had lots of fun doing it.

Fun-to-Find Money-Savers:

Here is a sampling of fun discounts from anywhere and everywhere for mature travelers. Just pick the place where your next trip is scheduled, and see what deals you can find there.

✓ indicates best values for mature travelers.

Alabama—Visitors 55+ get 10% off admission to Bellingrath Gardens & Home south of Mobile. 334/973-2217.

American Express—Cardmembers who sign up for the Senior Card get $20 off annual $55 membership fee, receive certificates for slight additional senior discounts on Amtrak (20% vs. 15%), Club Meds ($200 off vs. $150 for others), September Days memberships ($7 off), Westin Hotels and others. 800/323-8300.

Arizona—Phoenix: Visitors 65+ to the Heard Museum get $1 off $5 admission price. 602/252-8848.

British Columbia—<u>Tofino</u>: Jamie's Whaling Station gives seniors $5 off two- or three-hour $65 whale-watching trips from Vancouver Island. 604/725-3919.

<u>Vancouver</u>: Visitors 65+ get $1.45 off $14.95 round-trip fare on Grouse Mountain Tramway. 604/984-0661 . . . Visitors 60+ to Canada Craft Museum get half off $4 admission. 604/687-8266 . . . Seniors get $1 off $10 summer carriage tours of Stanley Park. 604/681-5115 . . . UCB Museum of Anthropology gives visitors 60+ $2.50 off $6 admission. 604/822-3825 . . . UCB Botanical Garden gives $2.25 off $4.25 admission. 604/822-4208 . . . Seniors get $1 off $7 550-foot glass elevator ride to The Lookout atop Harbour Centre. 604/689-0421 . . . 49ers+ get $1.85 off $6.10 admission to Burnaby's Heritage Village and Carousel. 604/293-6500 . . . Visitors 60+ get one-third of $6 admission to Vancouver Art Gallery. 604/682-4668 . . . B.C. Sports Hall of Fame gives seniors $2 off $6 adult

Fun Deals

admission. 604/687-5520.

Victoria: Travelers 65+ get $10 off $83 round-trip fare on Victoria Clipper between Seattle and Victoria. 800/888-2535.

California—Campers 62+ get $2 off admissions and overnight camping in state parks. Show ID at gate. Call 800/444-7275 for reservations . . . Visitors 62+ to Yosemite National Park get $4 off $44 sightseeing tours. 209/658-8687.

Anaheim: Visitors 60+ get $4 off $34 daily admission to Disneyland. 714/999-4565 . . . Knotts Berry Farm gives visitors 60+ $10 off regular $29 admission before 4 p.m. 714/220-5200.

Carmel—"Carmel Escape for Seniors" coupon book offers visitors 65+ savings on lodging, golf and attractions on the Monterey Peninsula. Contact Carmel Business Association, P.O. Box 4444, Carmel, CA 93921. 800/550-4333.

Coronado: Visitors 55+ get $2 off $17 tours of San Diego Harbor, departing the Coronado Pier. 619/437-8877.

Fresno: Three Piccadilly Inns give guests 65+ $94-$104 rooms for $65. 800/468-3522.

Gualala: AARP members get 10% off $125-$235 rooms at The Breakers Inn. 707/884-3200.

Lake Tahoe—Golfers 60+ get $10 off $67 green fees (including cart) at Northstar-at-Tahoe course. 916/562-2490. *(Also see Nevada listings.)*

Long Beach: Visitors 55+ get $2 off $10 adult admission to Queen Mary Seaport in Long Beach, Calif. 310/435-3511 . . . Seaport Marina Hotel, near the Queen Mary, gives guests 55+ 20% off rooms. 310/434-8451 . . . Airport Marriott "Senior Sunday" package gives travelers 55+ a $72 room plus dinner for two for $59. 310/425-5210 . . . Skirball Culture Center, Jewish history museum, gives 49ers+ $2 off regular $6 admission . . . 310/440-4500.For a *Senior Saver Getaway Guide* listing other senior discounts in Long Beach, call the convention and visitors bureau, 800/452-7829.

Los Angeles: Visitors 65+ get $2 off $6 admission to the Museum of Contemporary Art. 213/626-6222 . . . Deals at Marina del Rey include those at Doubletree, where guests 55+ get $210 rooms for $99 (800/222-8733); Marina del Rey Hotel, where guests 55+

get 25% discounts on $145-$170 rooms (310/301-1000); Marina International Hotel, where guests 65+ get $120 rooms for $89 (310/301-2000); and at two restaurants, Akbar Cuisine (25% off) and The Red Onion (20% off) . . . Mayfair Hotel, downtown, gives 49ers+ $80 rooms for $65. 800/821-8682 . . . 49ers+ get $190 rooms for $140 at Kimpton's Beverly Prescott hotel. 800/421-3212 . . . Visitors 65+ get $3.50 off $6 admission to La Brea Tar Pits (George C. Page Museum of La Brea Discoveries). 213/857-6311 . . . Visitors 60+ to Museum of Miniatures get $1 off regular $7.50 admission. 213/937-6464 . . . Simon Weisenthal Museum of Tolerance gives $2 off $8 admission fee to visitors 62+.310/553-8403 . . . Visitors 60+ get $5 off $34 Universal Studios tour. 818/622-8687 . . . *(Also see listings for California cities of Anaheim, Long Beach, Newport Beach, Pasadena, Van Nuys.)*

Monterey: Visitors 65+ get $2 off regular $13.75 admission price to Monterey Bay Aquarium. 408/648-4888 . . . Guests 55+ get 10% off room rates at Monterey Hotel, 800/727-0960 . . . Mariposa Motor Inn gives 10% discounts to guests 60+. 800/824-2295 . . . Sand Dollar Inn, near Fisherman's Wharf, gives AARP members 10% off $65-$75 rooms. 800/982-1986.

Newport Beach: Four Seasons Hotel gives travelers 65+ room discounts of 20%-to-40%. 800/332-3442 . . . Passengers 65+ get 10% discounts on Hornblower Dining Yachts' Sunday brunch and weekend dinner-dance cruises. 714/646-0155 . . . 49ers+ get $10 off $50 harbor cruises from Adventures at Sea. 800/229-2412 . . . $1 off $6 sunset cruises from Fun Zone Boat Co. 714/673-0240 . . . Half off $4 admission to the Newport Harbor Art Museum. 714/759-1122.

Palm Springs: Seniors get $4 off $49 Desert Adventures tram and jeep tours. 619/864-6530 . . . Visitors 55+ get $3 off $16.95 Mt. San Jacinto aerial tramway fare. 619/325-1449 . . . Visitors 62+ get $1 off, grandkids 3-12 get $3.50 off regular $7 admission price to The Living Desert. 619/346-5694 . . . Guests 55+ pay $80 for rooms that regularly cost $125-$140 a night at Erawan Garden Resort. The deal includes breakfasts and early-bird dinners. 800/234-2926 . . . 49ers+ get $20 off $55 chuckwagon cookout on Saturdays from Covered Wagon Tours. 619/347-2161.

Fun Deals

Pasadena: Heritage Square Museum gives 49ers+ $1 off $5 admission; 818/449-0193 . . . 49ers+ get $1.50 off regular $7.50 admission to Huntington Library. 818/405-2100 . . . Norton Simon Museum gives seniors half off $4 admission. 818/449-6840 . . . 49ers+ get $2 off $5 admission at both L.A. County Arboretum (818/821-3222) and Descanso Gardens (818/793-3334) . . . Seniors get $1 off $4 admission to Pasadena Historical Society/Feynes Estate. 818/577-1660.

Riverside: Historic Mission Inn gives AARP members 40% off rooms that regularly cost $105 to $155. 800/843-7755.

San Diego: Riders 60+ pay 75¢ on Tijuana Trolley, whose regular fares range up to $1.75 . . . LaPacifica Hotel downtown gives guests 55+ $10 off $49.95 rooms. 619/236-9292 . . . Guests 55+ get half off regular $160 room rate at Pala Mesa Resort in San Diego County wine country. 800/722-4700 . . . *(Also see Coronado entry.)*

San Francisco: See Chapter 10.

Santa Catalina: Passengers 55+ get $3.50 off $36 round-trip fares on Catalina Express boat to the island from Long Beach and San Pedro. 310/519-1212 . . . Seniors also get small discounts—$1 to $1.75—on island tours like the Glass Bottom Boat, the Casino, Back-Island Bus Tour, Starlight Drive Tram Ride and so on. 310/510-2500 . . . Almost all island inns give seniors 10% off room rates. Best deal in winter and spring seasons is at Cloud 7 Hotel (guests 65+ get 20% off $119 rooms weekdays—800/422-6836). For all island reservations call 310/510-2500.

Van Nuys: Travelers 65+ get $119 rooms for $79 at Airtel Plaza Hotel, 7277 Valjean Ave., Van Nuys, CA 91406. 818/997-7676.

Canada—National parks give visitors 65+ $1 off regular admission, which ranges from $2-to-$5 . . . Greyhound Lines of Canada gives 10% off trans-Canada bus fares to travelers 60+. 403/265-9111 . . . *(Also see listings for individual provinces.)*

Connecticut—Norwalk: Visitors 62+ get $1 off

$7.50 admission to Maritime Center. 203/852-0700.

Delaware—Visitors 62+ to Winterthur Museum, in the Brandywine Valley northwest of Wilmington, get $2 off $8 admission. 302/888-4600.

District of Columbia—John F. Kennedy Center for the Performing Arts charges half price on tickets for most performances to visitors 65+. 202/467-4600 . . . 1,700 restaurants, inns, merchants and other attractions listed in *Gold Mine Directory* give discounts to visitors 60+. Write D.C. Committee to Promote Washington, 1212 New York Ave NW #200, Washington, DC 20005; call 202/347-2873.

Europe—Thirty SAS International Hotels give guests 65+ percentage discounts equal to their ages. 800/221-230 . . . Travelers 60+ get $20-$50 discounts on Kouni Tours of Switzerland, Austria and Germany that normally cost $720 up. 800/346-6525.

Florida—See Chapter 10.

Golf—Golfers 62+ get 10% discounts off four-day or weekend instruction packages, including lodging and meals, at John Jacobs Golf Schools around the country from July through December. 800/472-5007.

Greyhound Lines—Travelers 55+ get 15% off all bus fares. 800/231-2222.

Hawaii—See Chapter 10.

Hong Kong—Free "60+ Privilege Cards" give visitors 60+ half off tour prices, 10-to-20% off meals and deep discounts on other attractions and shopping. With the cards, visitors get free rides on Star Ferry and pay half-price on inter-island ferries, subway, trams and other public transit. For a card, contact Hong Kong Tourist Assn., 590 Fifth Ave., 5th Floor, New York, NY 10036 (call 212/840-1690) or other H.K.T.A. offices in Chicago or Los Angeles. You can get a card when you arrive at H.K.T.A. airport kiosk, or at several kiosks around the city.

Idaho—Warren River Expeditions gives 49ers+ 10% discounts on Salmon River white-water trips; 208/756-6387 . . . 49ers+ get 15% off three-to-six day Main Salmon rafting trips from Mackay Adventure Travel. 800/635-5336.

Fun Deals

✓ **Oregon River Experiences hosts six-day Elderhostel whitewater trips, costing $365 a person, for rafters 55+—about half the regular cost of float trips. 503/697-8133.**

Boise: Travelers 62+ get 50¢ off $6.50 fare for Boise Tour Train historical tour. 208/342-4796.

Illinois—Chicago: Adler Planetarium gives visitors 65+ half off $4 admission. 312/322-0300 . . . Brookfield Zoo visitors 65+ and their grandkids get $3 off $5.50 admission. 708/485-2200 . . . Shedd Aquarium admits visitors 64+ for $2 off $10 price. 312/939-2438 . . . Visitors 65+ get $2 off $5 admission to Field Museum of Natural History. 312/922-9410 . . . Visitors 65+ get $1.25 off $5.75 admission to John Hancock Center Observatory. 312/751-3681 . . . Visitors 65+ get $1 off $3 admission at Chicago Academy of Sciences (312/549-0606) and Chicago Historical Society (312/642-4600).

Oak Park: Visitors 65+ get $2 off $6 admission to Frank Lloyd Wright Home & Studio. 708/848-1500.

Indiana—Santa Claus: Visitors 60+ get $6 off $18.95 admission to Holiday World & Splashin' Safari theme park. 800/467-2682.

Iowa—Des Moines: Visitors 60+ get $1 off $7 admission to Living History Farms. 515/278-5286.

✓ **Japan—Seniors Abroad annual three-week program for 49ers+ features homestays with three different families, costs under $3,000—an inexpensive way to visit high-priced Japan. 619/485-1696.**

Kentucky—Louisville: Passengers 60+ get $1 off $8 Belle of Louisville sternwheeler cruises, which run from Memorial Day to Labor Day. 502/723-3825 . . . Travelers 55+ get $1 off $4 admission to Kentucky Derby Museum. 502/723-3825 . . . The Seelbach grand hotel gives 49ers+ 25% off $142 rooms. 800/333-3399.

Louisiana—New Orleans: Travelers 62+ get half off Friends of Cabildo's $10 walking tour of historic French Quarter.

504/523-3939 . . . Visitors 55+ get $3 off $14.75 riverfront tour aboard the steamboat Natchez. 800/233-2628 . . . Visitors 62+ get $1 off admission to Beauregard-Keyes House. 504/523-7257 . . . Visitors 62+ get $1 off $6 Superdome Tours (504/587-3810).

Maine—49ers+ get free admission to state parks and historic sites with Senior Citizen Pass. To get a pass, just show proof of age at the gate. 207/287-3821.

Maryland—Baltimore: Visitors 60+ get $1 off $6 admission to B&O Railroad Museum. 410/752-2490 . . . 49ers+ get $2 off $5 admission to Babe Ruth Museum. 410/727-1539.

Massachusetts—Boston: Mature travelers get $4 off $16, narrated 90-minute Old Town Trolley Tours. 617/269-7010 . . . Seniors get $2 off $6 admission to the John F. Kennedy Museum. 617/929-4523 . . . 49ers+ get $1.50 off $7 admission to the Boston Tea Party Ship & Museum. 617/338-1773 . . . Museum of Fine Arts gives 49ers+ $2 off regular $8 admission. 617/267-9300 . . . At New England Aquarium on Central Wharf, seniors get $5 off regular $24 admission. 617/973-5200 . . . Visitors 62+ get $1 off $4 admission to USS Constitution Museum at Charleston Navy Yard; 617/426-1812 . . . 49ers+ get $3 off $18 "Ducks" tour of Charleston River, Back Bay, Beacon Hill. 617/723-3825 . . . Bay State Cruises gives visitors 62+ $7 off $29 day-long Provincetown cruises, $1 off shorter $5 Boston Harbor tours. 617/723-7800.

Old Sturbridge, re-created New England village, gives seniors $1.50 off $7 admission. 508/347-3362 . . . At Concord, 49ers+ get $1 off $5.50 admission to Orchard House, home of Louisa May Alcott. 508/369-4118 . . . Concord Museum gives seniors $1 off $5 admission.

Mexico--Center for Bilingual Studies in Cuernavaca gives students 55+ 10% off $350 tuition for two-week language sessions. 800/426-4660 . . . AARP members get 25% of $62 rooms at Grand Hotel Tijuana, just south of San Diego. 800/546-4030 . . . Lost World Trading gives travelers 55+ 5% off $735 Colonial Mexico tours. 209/847-5393.

Michigan—Detroit: Visitors 62+ get $1 off $12.50 admission to either Henry Ford Museum and Greenfield Village, $3 off $25 admission to both. 313/271-1620.

Ludington: Travelers 65+ get $3 off $35 fare aboard Lake Michigan Car Ferry from Ludington to Kewaunee,

Fun Deals

Wis. $55 round-trip costs seniors $50. 800/841-4243.

Travis City: Bayshore Resort gives travelers 60+ $75 rooms for $49 midweek, 25% off weekend rates. 800/634-4401.

Minnesota—Minneapolis: Guthrie Theater gives visitors 62+ $2 off tickets to all performances. 612/377-2224 . . . Visitors 65+ get $3 off $8 Minnesota Zoo admission. 612/432-9000.

St. Paul—49ers+ get $1 off $18 St. Paul Gangster Tours. 612/292-1220.

Mississippi—Gulfport: Seniors get $1 off $9.90 admission to Marine Life Oceanarium.

Missouri—St. Louis: Admission to Gateway Arch and Old Courthouse (314/425-4465) is free to travelers 62+ who hold Golden Age passports . . . Visitors 65+ get half-off $3 admission price to Missouri Botanical Gardens, America's oldest public botanical garden. 314/577-5100 . . . St. Louis Science Center in Forest Park, with free admission, gives visitors 60+ $1 off $5.50 shows at Omnimax Theater. 314/289-4400 . . . Museum of Transportation gives visitors 65+ $2.50 off regular $4 admission. 314/965-7998 . . . 49ers+ get 50¢ off one-hour, $7.50 riverfront sightseeing cruises aboard excursion boats run by Gateway Riverboat Cruises from Laclede's Landing. 314/621-4040 . . . The Magic House participatory museum gives visitors 55+ $1 off $3.50 admission. 314/822-8900 . . . 49ers+ get $1 off regular $4.50 admission to Bob Kramer's Marionettes puppet shows. 314/531-3313 . . . Visitors 60+ get half-off $2 admission to Cupples House historic home. 314/658-3025 . . . St. Louis Black Repertory Company gives visitors 60+ $5 off tickets for any main-stage performance, which vary in price. 314/534-3811 . . . Visitors 55+ get half-price tickets to St. Louis Symphony "Senior Sundays" performances. 314/534-2500 . . . 49ers+ get half off $28 admission to Six Flags Over Mid-America theme park in nearby Eureka. 314/938-4800 . . . Goldenrod Showboat at St. Charles, Mo., gives 49ers+ 10% discounts on most performances, ranging from Broadway revivals to off-Broadway plays. 314/946-2020 . . . Other deals for seniors are listed in St. Louis Sampler kit from St. Louis Convention & Visitors Commission, 800/325-7962.

Stanton: Visitors to Meramec Caverns get $1 off

regular $9 admission. 314/468-3166)

Montana—C.M. Russell Museum Complex in Great Falls gives 49ers+ $1 off $4 admission. 406/727-8787.

Nevada—Carson City: "Seniors Strike Silver" card and directory entitle 49ers+ to discounts at hundreds of motels, restaurants, casinos and other establishments in Nevada's capital city. 800/638-2321.

Lake Tahoe: 49ers+ get $4 off $26 dinner cruises aboard paddlewheeler M.S. Dixie II from Zephyr Cove. 702/882-0786. *(Also see California listings.)*

Las Vegas: See Chapter 10.

Reno: Holiday Inn hotel-casino on edge of downtown gives Mature Outlook members 20% off rooms, 10% off meals and car rentals; others 55+ get 10% discounts on rooms. 800/465-4329 . . . AARP members get 15% off Sierra Nevada Stage Lines guided tours. 702/331-2877.

New Hampshire—Dixville Notch: Balsams Grand Resort Hotel gives AARP members 10% off rooms and meals; also 10% off golf packages. 603/255-3400.

New Jersey—Camden: Visitors 65+ to New Jersey State Aquarium get $1.50 off regular $9.95 admission. 609/365-3300.

New Mexico—Visitors 62+ get $1 off $3 admission to Albuquerque's Pueblo Cultural Center museum. 505'843-7270
. . . Albuquerque Visitors Bureau publishes a free directory listing other senior discounts ranging from Sandia Peak tram to Civic Light Opera. 800/284-2282.

New York—New Paltz: 49ers+ taking part in New Paltz Summer Living Program, June through August every year, pay $1,200 to $3,200 total for furnished apartments, some meals, social activities and free college classes. 407/243-0811.

New York City: See Chapter 10.

North Carolina—Asheville: Grove Park Inn gives AARP members 10% discounts on rooms that range in price from $175 to $216. 800/438-5800.

Roanoke Island: Visitors 65+ get $2 off $14 admission to Friday performances of The Lost Colony, $1 off other performances. 800/488-5012.

Norway—Oslo: 49ers+ get $1.50 off $2.50 admis-

Fun Deals

sion to Resistance Museum.

Ohio—Canton: Visitors 62+ get half-off $4 admission price to Pro Football Hall of Fame. 216/456-8207.

Cincinnati: Visitors 65+ get various discounts on Mondays at the Museum Center, housing Cincinnati Historical Society, Museum of Natural History and Omnimax. 800/733-2077.

Middletown: Manchester Inn, near Cincinnati, gives guests 65+ 25% off rooms that are regularly $72. 800/523-9126.

Sandusky: Visitors 60+ get $13 off $28.95 admission price at Cedar Point amusement park. 419/627-2350.

Oklahoma—Oklahoma City: Visitors 62+ get $1 off $6.50 admission at National Cowboy Hall of Fame. 405/478-2250.

Ontario—Stouffville: Visitors 60+ get 25% off Sundance Balloons flights, regularly $119-$175 (CDN). 416/364-6804.

Toronto: Seniors get $5 (CDN) off $15 admission to Underground City Tours (905/886-9111), $2 off Neighborhood Walks, regularly $12-$25 (CDN). 416/463-9233 . . . 49ers+ get $2 off $6 admission to Bata Shoe Museum. 416/9797799 . . . Visitors 60+ to Paramount Canada's Wonderland theme park get half off $35.80 (CDN) admission. 905/832-7000 . . . Travelers 60+ get $11 off $95 day-long Niagara Falls tours. 416/594-3310 . . . Toronto Historical Board sites giving discounts to visitors 65+ include Fort York (416/392-6907), Mackenzie House (416/392-6915), Colburne Lodge (416/392-6916) and the Marine Museum (416/392-1765) . . . Visitors 65+ get $3 off $10 (CDN) admission to Metro Toronto Zoo. 416/392-5900 . . . Visitors 65+ get $2 off $8 (CDN) admission to Black Creek Pioneer Village. 416/736-1733 . . . Royal Ontario Museum gives 49ers+ $3 off regular $7 (CDN) admission, free admission on Tuesdays. 416/586-5549 . . . Visitors 60+ get $2.50 (CDN) off $9.95 self-guided Passport to Wine Country tours, plus discounts on meals, B&Bs and merchandise, from Niagara Winery Tour Company, which also gives seniors 10% off $79.95 (CDN) day-long guided tours of wineries. 416/256-5658.

AARP and CARP members get 30% off regular $139-$169 (CDN) rooms at Sky Dome Hotel, where some rooms overlook Blue Jays playing field. Other guests 65+ get 25% off rooms. 800/341-1161 . . . Royal York hotel gives AARP and CARP members 30% off rooms regularly priced at $229-309(CDN). 800/828-7447.

Oregon—Newport: Oregon Coast Aquarium gives visitors 65+ $1 off regular $8 admission. 541/867-3474.

Portland: 49ers+ get $155 rooms for $125 at Vintage Plaza hotel. 800/234-0555.

Pennsylvania—Chadds Ford: Brandywine River Museum, with collection of Wyeth family art, gives visitors 65+ half off $5 admission. 610/388-2700.

Hershey: Visitors 55+ to Hersheypark, including the chocolate factory, get $10.50 off $26.45 admission. 717/534-3900.

Langhorne: 49ers+ get $7 off $22.95 admission to Sesame Place park. 215/757-1100.

Philadelphia: Visitors 65+ who show ID ride off-peak hours free on regional trains, buses, trolleys and subway system . . . 49ers+ get $2.50 off $17.50 Riverpass Tickets good for admissions to Independence Seaport Museum and Historic Ship Zone, the New Jersey State Aquarium at Camden and round-trip ferry tickets between the two; $1.50 off $7.50 admission to the Museum. 215/925-5439 . . . Gray Line gives 49ers+ $2 off $18 half-day tours to Valley Forge, historic Philadelphia and cultural Philadelphia. 800/577-774) . . . Visitors 60+ get $5 off $20 guided tours of from Little Italy Tours. Call 215/334-6008 . . . Eastern State Penitentiary, 1820s prison, gives $2 off $7 admission to visitors 62+. 215/236-7236 . . . Visitors 55+ get 25% off food at ASA Cafe Japanese Bistro. 215/568-5995 . . . AARP members get 20% off food bill from 4 to 6 p.m. at Irish Pub. 215/925-3311 . . . Le Champignon gives guests 55+ 25% off food bill. 215/922-2515 . . . 49ers+ get 20% off meals at Marrakesh Moroccan restaurant. 215/925-5929 . . . Travelers 62+ get $3 off the $7 admission at the Museum of Art. 215/235-7469 . . . The Philadelphia Orchestra gives 49ers+ 10% "Visitors Discount" on all performances. 215/893-1900 . . . Museum of Archaeology & Anthropology at University of Pennsylvania gives

Fun Deals

visitors 62+ half off $5 admission. 215/898-4000 . . . Museum of American Art gives $1 off $5.95 admission to visitors 62+. 215/972-7600 . . . Franklin Institute Science Museum gives $1 off $9.50 admission to visitors 62+. 215/448-1200 . . . Visitors 65+ to Institute of Contemporary Art get $2 off $3 admission. 215/898-7108 . . . 49ers+ get 50¢ off $2.50 admission to Mummers Museum. 215/336-3050 . . . Visitors 62+ get half-off $4 admission to Afro-American Historical & Cultural Museum. 215/574-0380 . . . Visitors 60+ to National Museum of American Jewish History get 75¢ off $2.50 admission. 215/923-3812 . . . *Philadelphia Mature Travelers Discounts* booklet lists year-around discounts for 49ers+ at inns, attractions, restaurants, performances and transportation. Available at Visitors Center, 16th & John F. Kennedy Blvd., or by phone, 800/537-7676 . . . *(Also see Camden, N.J., entry.)*.

Strasburg: Visitors 60+ to the Railroad Museum of Pennsylvania get $1 off $6 admission.

Portugal—49ers+ pay an average $55 a night per room during off-season, October through June, at 37 *pousadas* booked by Marketing Ahead. 800/223-1356.

Quebec—Montreal: Travelers 65+ get $2 off $19.75 admission to Le Bateau-Mouche boat tours of the riverfront. For reservations, 514/849-9952.

Scotland—Travelers 60+ get up to one-third off day-long tours around Edinburgh and Glasgow from Personalized Tours. 011-01698-882084.

South Carolina—Charleston: Visitors 62+ get $1 off $5 admission to Gibbes Museum of Art downtown. 803/722-2706 . . . 49ers+ get $1 off $12 admission to Middleton Place plantation house and gardens. Call 803/556-6020 . . . Lowcountry Legends gives 49ers+ 10% off regular $18 show tickets. 803/722-1829 . . . Seniors get $1 off $9 admission to Patriots Point, featuring carrier Yorktown and other WWII ships. 803/884-2727 . . . Charleston Strolls gives 49ers+ $2 off $12.50 downtown walking tours. 803/884-9505 . . . 49ers+ get $2 off $10 downtown minibus tours by Tailored Tours of Charleston. 803/763-5747 . . . Gray Line gives 49ers+ $1 off $11.50 downtown minibus tours and $19.50 area tours. 800/423-0444 . . . Seniors get 50¢ off regular 75¢ fare on Downtown Area Shuttle (DASH) trolley tours. 803/724-7420 . . . Visitors 60+ get

$2 off $15 horse-drawn carriage tours from Olde Town Carriage Co. 803/722-1315 . . . Fort Sumter Tours gives visitors 62+ $1 off $9.50 harbor tour and boat trip to the fort. 803/722-1691 . . . Mills House hotel gives AARP members 10% off rooms that regularly range $135-$175. 800/874-9600 . . . Hawthorn Suites at the Market gives AARP members up to 30% off room rates, depending on season. 800/527-1133 . . . Embassy Suites gives 49ers+ $20 off $139-$269 rooms. 803/723-6900 . . . Kiawah Island Resort gives AARP members 10% off rooms regularly priced $125-$195. 803/768-2121 . . . Hotels that honor their parent chains' senior-discount plans include Days Inn, Comfort Inn, Howard Johnson, Quality Inn and Sheraton (see Chapter 2).

Spain—Travelers 60+ get up to 50% off *paradors* taking part in "Golden Years" plan. 800/223-1356.

Switzerland—More than 380 hotels in 160 Swiss towns offer off-season rates for women over 62, men over 65. Switzerland Tourism, 608 Fifth Ave., New York, NY 10020; call 212/757-5944.

Tennessee—Travelers 62+ with Golden Age Pass or Golden Access Pass get 50% off entrance fees and camping at Tennessee state parks. 615/532-0001.

Florence: Cross Country Inn, across the river from Cincinnati, gives AARP members and others 60+ 25% discounts off $47 rooms. 606/283-2030.

Memphis: Visitors 60+ to Mud Island get $8 admission for $6. 901/576-7241 . . . 49ers+ get $1 off $9 admission to historic Hunt-Phelan home on Beale Street. 800/350-9009.

Texas—Dallas: The Sixth Floor, Kennedy assassination museum, gives visitors 65+ half off $6 admission. 214/653-6666 . . . Visitors 55+ get $6 off $30 admission to Six Flags Over Texas theme park. 817/640-8900.

Houston: Visitors 65+ get $1 off $4 tours of the Astrodome. 713/799-9555.

San Antonio: Visitors 55+ get 10% off $27 admission to Sea World. 210/523-3000 . . . Visitors 55+ get one-third off $27.95 admission at Fiesta Texas. 800/473-4378 . . . Historic Menger Hotel downtown gives

Fun Deals 127

guests 55+ and AARP members $142 rooms for $80. 800/345-9285 . . . Guests 60+ get 10% off $142 rooms at the St. Anthony Hotel. 210/227-4392 . . . 49ers+ get $185 rooms at Fairmount Hotel for $145. 800/642-3363.

✓ **U. S. National Parks**—Travelers 62+ pay a $10 for Golden Age pass, good for lifetime free admission to national parks and wildlife refuges, plus 50% discounts on park user fees, like overnight RV camping. Apply in person at offices of National Park Service, Fish & Wildlife, Forest Service, BLM, Bureau of Reclamation, TVA or Army Engineers. Call 800/365-2267 for camping reservations.

Virginia—Charlottesville: Visitors 60+ get $1 off $8 admission to Monticello, Jefferson's home. 804/984-9822.

Newport News: Visitors 60+ get $1 off $6.50 admission to The Marner's Museum. 804/596-2222.

Norfolk: Visitors 60+ get $1 off $10.95 admission to Nauticus maritime center. 800/664-1080.

Virginia Beach—Travelers 55+ asking for "AARP Rate" at The Founders Inn get rooms on weeknights, normally $150 in high season, for $85 a night. 800/926-4466.

Williamsburg: Williamsburg Pottery Factory outlet stores give shoppers 60+ 10% discounts Monday-Thursday. 804/564-3326 . . . Guests 55+ get $3 off $29.95 admission to Busch Gardens and $2 off $21.95 admission to Water Country USA.

Washington—Passengers 65+ get half off fares that range from $3.50 to $5 on Washington State Ferries. 206/464-6400.

Bellingham: Inn at Semi-Ah-Moo gives mature travelers discounts from $125 room rate equal to their age October through June. 800/770-7992

Deming: 49ers+ get $2 off $5 admission to annual Deming Logging Show each June.

Seattle: See Chapter 10.

Wisconsin—Kewaunee: Travelers 65+ get $3 off $35 fare aboard Lake Michigan Car Ferries from Kewaunee to Ludington, Mich. 800/841-4243.

Spring Green: Visitors 62+ get $5 off $30 guided tours of Taliesin, Frank Lloyd Wright's studio and home on Tuesday and Thursday. 608/588-7900.

<u>Wisconsin Dells</u>: 49ers+ carrying a "Wis. Dells Senior Discount Card" get 10-20% off several attractions in the Upper and Lower Dells of the Wisconsin River. Write Dells Associated Boat Lines, P.O. Box 208-C, Wisconsin Dells, WI 53965.

Wyoming—<u>Cody</u>: Visitors 62+ get $1.50 off $8 admission to Buffalo Bill Historical Center. 307/587-4771.

<u>Jackson</u>: Visitors 50+ get $1 off $4 admission to National Museum of Wildlife Art. 307/733-5771.

<u>Thermopolis</u>: Visitors 60+ get $3 off $10 tours through Jurassic Era dig sites at new Wyoming Dinosaur Center, also $2.50 off $6 admission to the center's museum. 800/455-3466. ❑

A Deal for Your Deals

By the way, we want to hear about any great new discounts for mature travelers that you find. If they check out, we'll give you $5 off a regular $29.95 subscription to *The Mature Traveler* newsletter.

Write us at TMT Deals, P.O. Box 50400, Reno, NV 89513-0400.

Tell us the discount, the regular price for adults, how old you have to be, the phone number and address of the hotel, tour or attraction giving the discount.

And when you write us for your subscription, be sure to ask for the discount.

--Gene & Adele Malott
Editors of *The Mature Traveler* Newsletter

Index
To the Deals

A

Admiral Benbow Inns 23
Affordable Travel Club, Inc. 13
Air Canada 39
Air Courier Association 38
Air couriers 37
Air Tickets 37
Airfare consolidators 34
Airline senior "passports" 32, 33
Airline senior-discount coupons 32
Alabama 114
Alamo Rent-A-Car 56, 60
Alaska 104
Alaska Airlines 39
Alaska Marine Highway 54
Alaska Railroad 66
America West 39
American Airlines 40, 45
American Association of Retired Persons (AARP) 4, 55
American Express 114
American Hiking Society 97
American International Homestays (AIH) 14
American Queen 53
American Youth Hostels 18
American-International Homestays (AIH) 14
Amtrak 61
Amtrak All Aboard America Fares 62, 66
Arizona 114
Aston "Sun Club" 23, 103
Avis Rent A Car 60

B

Bahamas 105
Ballroom Dancers Without Partners 49, 87
Bereavement airfares 34
Bergen Line 54
Best Inns 23
Best of Cross Country Skiing, The 73
Best Western 23

Boston 120
Breckenridge "50-Plus Seminars" 71
Breckenridge "Senior Games of the Summit" 71
British Columbia 114
BritRail Senior Passes 63, 67
Budget Car Rental 60
Budget Lodging Guide 17
Budgetel 23

C

California 115
Campus stays 17
Canada national parks 117
Canadian Airlines 40
Canadian Association of Retired Persons (CARP) 5, 55
Canadian Pacific Hotels 23
Canrail Pass 63, 66
Caribbean 104
Carte Vermeil 67
Cascade Lodge 73
Castle Resorts 23
Cheap Seats 35, 37
Cheap Tickets, Inc. 35, 37
Chicago 119
Choice Hotels 24
Chunnel Train 67
Club Med 2 49
Colony Hotels & Resorts 24
Condo & Villa Vacations Rated Guides 18
Condo rentals 18
Condolink 18
Connecticut 117
Consumer Reports Travel Letter 58
Continental Airlines 40
Continental Freedom Passport 40
Cooper Communities 14
Costa Cruises 54
Counselor Recruitment Handbook 95
Country Hearth 24
Country Inns 24
Courtyard by Marriott 24
Cranmore "Heritage Program" 71
Creative Leisure International 18

Index

Cross Country Inns 24
Cross Country Ski Areas Association 73
Cross-country ski deals 80
Cross-country skiing 73
Crown Sterling Suites 25
Cruise Line, Inc., The 49, 50
Cruise specialists 49, 50
Cruiseship jobs 99
Crystal Cruises 53
Crystal Mountain, Mich. 71, 73
CUC Travel Services 51
Cunard Lines 52, 53

D

Days Inns 25
Del Webb's Sun Cities 14
Delaware 118
Delta Air Lines 41
Delta Queen Steamboat Co. 49, 53
Delta Shuttle 41
District of Columbia 118
Dollar Rent A Car 60
Doubletree Inns & Guest Quarters 25
Downhill ski deals 75
Drury Inns 25

E

EF Educational Tours 95
Elderhostel 73, 88, 93, 119
Embassy Suites 25
Empty-seat theory 3
Encore 17
Enterprise Rent-A-Car 60
Entertainment Publications (EP) 16
EurailPass 64
Euram 37
Europak Scan 37
Eurostar trains 64
Excel Inns 25

F

Fairfield Inns by Marriott 25
Fitzgerald's Casino/Hotel 21, 108

Florida 105
Friendship Inns 25
Frontier Airlines 42
Frontier Travel & Tours 96

G

Gentleman hosts 52, 89
Global Discount Travel Services 35, 37
Golden Companions 84
Grand Circle Travel 48, 49, 86, 95
Grandkids-stay-free 9
Great Britain 102
Group Leaders of America 95
Group tour leaders 94

H

Hale Koa 15
Harley Hotels 25
Hawaii 102
Hawaiian Air 42
Helping Out in the Outdoors 97
Hertz Rent A Car 60
Hilton International 26
Hilton Senior HHonors Club 6, 25
Holiday Inns Alumni Club 6, 26
Holland America 53
Home swapping 19
Homestays 13
Homewood Suites 26
Hong Kong 60+ Privilege Cards 118
Hosteling 17
Hostelship scholarships 93
Howard Johnson's Golden Years Club 6, 26
Hyatt Hotels 26

I

Idaho 118
I'm Proud To Be Me Travel 49
Indiana 119
Inn Suites 26
Innkeeper motels 26
Interhostel 88
International airfare discounts 32, 46

Index

International Association of Air Travel
     Couriers (IAATC) 37
Intervac U.S. 19
Iowa 119
Ireland 102
ITC-50 5, 17

J

Jetset 37
Jobs in travel 98

K

Kauai 103
Kentucky 119
Kimpton Group hotels 26
Kiwi International Airlines 42
Knights Inns 27

L

La Quinta Motor Inns 27
Lanikai Cruises 54
Las Vegas 107
Last-minute travel clubs 50
Late-in-the-day lodging discounts 12
Lauretta Blake's The Working Vacation 53, 100
Lodgekeeper and LK Inns 27
Lodging discounts 20
London 107
Lone Star Airlines 42
Lookout Pass "Boomer Days" 71

M

Maine 120
Marc Resorts 27
Marriott Hotels 27
Mature Outlook club 5, 55
Mature Tours 49, 87
Mature Travelers' Favorite Places ballot 111
Mature Traveler newsletter 2, 50, 101, 128
Mature Traveler reader survey 101
Maui 103
Merry Widows 53, 87
Mexico 120

Michigan 120
Mid-week lodging discounts 12
Midwest Express 42
Military hotels 15
Military Living Publications 15
Minnesota 121
Mississippi 121
Mississippi Queen 53
Montana 122
Montreal 125
Motel 6 27
Mt. Baker International 66

N

National Car Rental 60
Nevada 122
New Hampshire 122
New Jersey 122
New Mexico 122
New Orleans 119
New York City 109
New York State 122
New Zealand 104
Nickels and Dimes discounts 113
No-frills airlines 38
North Carolina 122
Northstar "Golden Stars Ski Clinics" 72
Northwest Airlines 42, 45
Norway 122
Novotel 27

O

Oahu 104
Off-season room discounts 11
Ohio 123
Oklahoma 123
Omni Hotels 27
Ontario Northland 66
Oregon 124
Orient Line 53
Outdoor volunteers 96
Outrigger Hotels 28
Over The Hill Gang 70

Index

P

Paris 107
Park Inns 28
Partners For Travel 84
Partners In Travel 85
Payless "Nifty Fifty Club" 60
Peabody Orlando 21
Pennsylvania 124
Philadelphia 124
Polar Bear Express 66
Portugal 125
Positioning cruises 51
Preferred Travelers Club 17
Premier Cruise Lines 54
Privilege Card 17
Prussian Princess 87
Puerto Rico 105

R

Radisson Hotels 28
Rail Europe 65
Ramada Best Years Club 28
Ramada International 28
Red Lion Inns 28
Red Roof Inns 28
Renaissance Hotels & Resorts 28
Reno Air 43
Residence Inns by Marriott 28
Restaurant discounts 9
Retirement Villas 14
Rodeway Inns 28
Royal Cruise Lines 51, 52
Royal Hawaiian Cruises 54

S

Saga Holidays 86
San Francisco 106
Sandman Motels 28
SAS International Hotels 118
Scanrail 55+ Pass 65, 68
Schweitzer Mountain "Prime Timers Club" 72
Scotland 125
Seattle 109

Index

Senior Shucks 6
Senior Travel Recreation and Activities Council (STRAC) 95
Senior Vacation Hotels 21
"Senior-friendly" rooms 10
Seniors Abroad 13, 119
September Days Club 25
Seventy-Plus Ski Club 70
Sheraton Hotels 29
Shilo Inns 29
Shoney's Merit 50 Club 29
Silja Line 54
Silver Sea Cruises 53
Silver Streaks 73
Silver Striders Golden Gliders 73
Silver Wings Plus Travel Club 44
Single-share programs 85
Single-supplement penalties 83
Singleworld Tours 86
Sir Francis Drake 54
Sky Dome Hotel 22
Skylink 37
Snowbird "Senior Seminar" 72
Solo-friendly cruiselines 89
South Florida Cruises 51
Southwest Airlines 43
Spain 125
St. Louis 121
Summerfield Suites 29
Sun Cities 14
Sun Valley "Prime Time Specials" 72
Susse Chalets 29
Switzerland 125

T

Tennessee 125
Texas 126
TGIF ("Thank Goodness I'm Fifty" ski club) 71
Thrifty Car Rental 56, 60
Toronto 123
Trading Homes International 19
Travac 37
Travel Companion Exchange (TCE) 85
Travel Industry Association of America (TIA) 55

Index

Travel jobs 98
Travel matchmakers 84
Travelodge 29
Turks & Caicos 105
TWA 43

U

U. S. National Parks 126
Union Jack Club 15
Unique World Travel 54
United Air Lines 43
United Shuttle 44
USAir 44, 45
USAir Shuttle 44

V

Vacation Exchange Club 19
Vacations to Go 50
Vagabond Inns 29
Value Rent-A-Car 60
Value World Tours 54
Verde Canyon Railroad 66
Via Rail 63, 66
Victory Services Club 15
Virginia 126

W

Washington 126
Weekend lodging discounts 12
Welcome Inns 29
Westin Hotels 29
Wild Old Bunch 70
Wisconsin 127
Workcamper News 99
World Explorer cruises 53, 87
World of Cruising Magazine 50
Worldwide Discount Travel Club 51
Wyndham Hotels & Resorts 29
Wyoming 127

Y

Y.E.S. Discount Club 5

About the Authors:

Gene and Adele Malott have been America's leading observers of the senior travel scene for more than 10 years. Authors of The Mature Traveler column, distributed weekly by The New York Times Syndicate to major daily newspapers, and editors of <u>The Mature Traveler</u> monthly newsletter, the Malotts regularly explore seniors' favorite destinations around the world.

In *The Mature Traveler's Book of Deals*, these veteran newspaper and magazine journalists share with readers what they have learned on their travels: the best discounts going for 49ers+, great trips and tours for mature travelers, and the world's most senior-friendly places.